Math in Focus

Singapore Math
by Marshall Cavendish

Reteach

Author

Melvin Teo

Marshall Cavendish
Education

U.S. Distributor

Houghton
Mifflin
Harcourt

COMMON CORE

© 2013 Marshall Cavendish International (Singapore) Private Limited
© 2014 Marshall Cavendish Education Pte Ltd

Published by Marshall Cavendish Education
Times Centre, 1 New Industrial Road, Singapore 536196
Customer Service Hotline: (65) 6213 9444
U.S. Office Tel: (1-914) 332 8888 | Fax: (1-914) 332 8882
E-mail: tmesales@mceducation.com
Website: www.mceducation.com

Distributed by
Houghton Mifflin Harcourt
222 Berkeley Street
Boston, MA 02116
Tel: 617-351-5000
Website: www.hmheducation.com/mathinfocus

Cover: © Tim Laman/Getty Images

First published 2013

Math in Focus® Reteach Course 2A
ISBN 978-0-547-57883-5

Printed in Singapore

5 6 7 8   1401   17 16 15
4500546152   B C D E

Contents

Introducing Math in Focus® Reteach

Reteach, written to complement ***Math in Focus®: Singapore Math® by Marshall Cavendish***, offers a second opportunity to practice skills and concepts at the entry level. Key vocabulary terms are explained in context, complemented by sample problems with clearly worked-out solutions.

For On-Level Students

Not all students can master a new concept or skill after the first practice. A second opportunity to practice at the same level before moving on can be key to long-term success for these students.

For Below-Level Students

Monitor students' levels of understanding during daily instruction and as they work on Practice exercises. Provide *Reteach* worksheets to struggling students who would benefit from further practice at a basic level. The worksheets can also be used to remediate specific problems on the Chapter Tests, Benchmark Test, or Mid-Course Test.

 Reteach is also available online and on the Teacher One Stop.

Credits

CHAPTER

1 The Real Number System

Lesson 1.1 Representing Rational Numbers on the Number Line

Order the numbers from least to greatest. Use the < symbol. Graph each number on a horizontal number line.

1. $\frac{10}{3}$, $1\frac{1}{2}$, 0.4, 0.9

2. 0.23, $\frac{1}{4}$, $\frac{4}{3}$, $\frac{5}{8}$

Compare. Write <, >, or =.

3. 2.12 ⬜ 2.31

4. 0.37 ⬜ 0.317

Round each number.

5. 2,549 to the nearest ten. _____

6. 23.17 to 1 decimal place. _____

Round 7,363.923

7. to the nearest hundredth. _____

8. to the nearest whole number. _____

Find the square and cube of each number.

9. 7

10. 10

Find the square root of each number.

11. 36

12. 81

Find the cube root of each number.

13. 125   **14.** 512

Order the numbers from greatest to least. Use the > symbol.

15. 2^2, $\sqrt{100}$, 3^3 **16.** 2^3, 4^2, $\sqrt{16}$

Complete each inequality using >, =, or <.

17. $|21|$ ⬜ $|-21|$ **18.** $|8|$ ⬜ $|-88|$

Find the absolute values of fractions.

--- Example ---

a) Find the absolute values of $-\dfrac{5}{6}$ and $\dfrac{3}{4}$.

$\left|-\dfrac{5}{6}\right| = \dfrac{5}{6}$ and $\left|\dfrac{3}{4}\right| = \dfrac{3}{4}$

b) Using a number line, show how far $-\dfrac{5}{6}$ and $\dfrac{3}{4}$ are from 0. Which number is closer to 0?

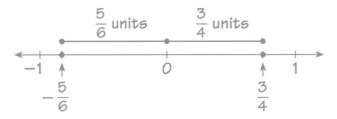

$-\dfrac{5}{6}$ is ___$\dfrac{5}{6}$___ units to the left of 0.

$\dfrac{3}{4}$ is ___$\dfrac{3}{4}$___ units to the right of 0.

Because the distance $\dfrac{5}{6}$ units $> \dfrac{3}{4}$ units, ___$\dfrac{3}{4}$___ is closer to 0.

Name: _____   Date: _____

Complete.

19. a) Find the absolute values of $2\frac{2}{3}$ and $-\frac{9}{4}$.

$$\left|2\frac{2}{3}\right| = \underline{\hspace{1.5cm}} \quad \text{and} \quad \left|-\frac{9}{4}\right| = \underline{\hspace{1.5cm}}$$

b) Graph the two numbers on a number line and indicate their distances from 0. Which number is farther from 0?

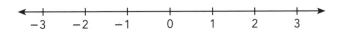

_____ is farther from 0.

Solve.

20. a) Find the absolute values of $-\frac{5}{8}$ and $\frac{2}{3}$.

b) Graph the two numbers on a number line and indicate their distances from 0. Which number is farther from 0?

21. a) Find the absolute values of $1\frac{1}{4}$ and $-\frac{11}{6}$.

b) Graph the two numbers on a number line and indicate their distances from 0. Which number is farther from 0?

Name: _____   Date: _____

Write each number in $\frac{m}{n}$ form where *m* and *n* are integers.

Example

a) $-2\frac{6}{7}$

$$-2\frac{6}{7} = -\left(\frac{2\cdot 7}{7} + \frac{6}{7}\right)$$
$$= -\frac{20}{7}$$

b) 19

$$19 = \frac{19}{1}$$

Whole numbers have 1 in the denominator.

Complete.

22. $3\frac{4}{6}$

$$3\frac{4}{6} = \frac{\boxed{} \cdot \boxed{}}{6} + \frac{\boxed{}}{6}$$

$$= \text{_____}$$

$$= \text{_____}$$

23. -17

$$-17 = \frac{-\boxed{}}{1} \text{ or } = \frac{\boxed{}}{-1}$$

Write each number in $\frac{m}{n}$ form where *m* and *n* are integers.

24. $-\frac{15}{10}$

25. $1\frac{12}{18}$

26. $-4\frac{2}{3}$

27. $1\frac{9}{21}$

Write each decimal in $\frac{m}{n}$ form where m and n are integers with $n \neq 0$.

Example

a) 0.6

$0.6 = \dfrac{6}{10}$ 6 is in the tenths place. Use 10 as the denominator.

$= \dfrac{3}{5}$ Simplify.

b) −0.25

$-0.25 = -\dfrac{25}{100}$ 5 is in the hundredths place. Use 100 as the denominator.

$= -\dfrac{1}{4}$ Simplify.

Complete.

28. 7.5

$7.5 = \boxed{}\,\dfrac{1}{\boxed{}}$ Write the integer, _____. Write 0.5 as _____.

$= \text{_____}$ Write as an improper fraction.

Write each decimal in $\frac{m}{n}$ form where m and n are integers with $n \neq 0$.

29. − 0.375

30. 3.6

31. − 9.36

32. 3.625

33. 3.21

34. − 1.045

Locate the following rational numbers on the number line.

Example

-1.6 and $\dfrac{5}{6}$

Step 1

Find the integers that the rational number lies between.

-1.6 is located between ___−2___ and ___−1___.

$\dfrac{5}{6}$ is a proper fraction so it is located between ___0___ and ___1___.

Step 2

Graph a number line and label the integers.

Step 3

Divide the distance between the integers into equal segments.

You divide the distance between 0 and 1 into 6 equal segments and the distance between -2 and -1 into 10 equal segments.

Step 4

Use the segments to locate -1.6 and $\dfrac{5}{6}$.

Name: _____ Date: _____

Complete.

35. $-\dfrac{1}{5}$ and $\dfrac{10}{4}$

Step 1
Find the integers that the rational number lies between.

$-\dfrac{1}{5}$ is a negative proper fraction so it is located between

_____ and _____ .

$\dfrac{10}{4}$ can be written as a mixed number, $2\dfrac{1}{2}$, and $2\dfrac{1}{2}$ lies between

_____ and _____ .

Step 2
Graph a number line and label the integers.

Step 3
Divide the distance between the integers into equal segments.

You divide the distance between −1 and 0 into _____ equal segments and

the distance between 2 and 3 into _____ equal segments.

Step 4
Use the segments to locate $-\dfrac{1}{5}$ and $\dfrac{10}{4}$.

Locate the following rational numbers on the number line.

36. $-\dfrac{5}{8}$ and 2.2

Lesson 1.2   Writing Rational Numbers as Decimals

Use long division to write rational numbers as terminating decimals.

┌─ *Example* ───┐

a) $\dfrac{5}{8}$

$$
\begin{array}{r}
0.625 \\
8\overline{)5.000} \\
\underline{48} \\
20 \\
\underline{16} \\
40 \\
\underline{40} \\
0
\end{array}
$$

Divide 5 by 8.
Add zeros after the decimal point.

The remainder is 0.

So, $\dfrac{5}{8} = 0.625$.

b) $2\dfrac{1}{4}$

$$
\begin{array}{r}
0.25 \\
4\overline{)1.00} \\
\underline{8} \\
20 \\
\underline{20} \\
0
\end{array}
$$

Divide 1 by 4.

Add zeros after the decimal point.

The remainder is 0.

So, $2\dfrac{1}{4} = 2.25$.

You could also write $2\dfrac{1}{4}$ as the mixed number $\dfrac{9}{4}$ and then divide: $9 \div 4$.

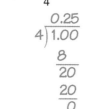

└──┘

1. $\dfrac{3}{25}$

2. $\dfrac{17}{16}$

Using long division, write each rational number as a terminating decimal.

3. $2\frac{1}{8}$

4. $\frac{9}{20}$

5. $\frac{3}{16}$

6. $\frac{18}{8}$

Use long division or a calculator to write rational numbers as repeating decimals.

┌─── *Example* ───┐

$\frac{7}{9}$

$$\begin{array}{r} 0.777 \\ 9\overline{)7.000} \\ \underline{63} \\ 70 \\ \underline{63} \\ 70 \\ \underline{63} \\ 7 \end{array}$$

Stop dividing when you see the digits repeat themselves.

So, $\frac{7}{9} = 0.777...$

└───┘

7. $\frac{6}{11}$

 8. $\frac{17}{15}$

Using long division, write each rational number as a repeating decimal. Use bar notation to indicate the repeating digits.

Example

$$\frac{5}{11}$$

$$\begin{array}{r} 0.4545 \\ 11\overline{)5.0000} \\ 44 \\ \hline 60 \\ 55 \\ \hline 50 \\ 44 \\ \hline 60 \\ 55 \\ \hline 5 \end{array}$$

So, $\frac{5}{11} = 0.4545... = 0.\overline{45}$.

The digits 4 and 5 form a repetitive group.

9. $\frac{2}{9}$

10. $\frac{30}{22}$

Using long division, write each rational number as a repeating decimal with 3 decimal places. Identify the pattern of repeating digits using bar notation.

11. $\frac{13}{6}$

12. $\frac{34}{33}$

Name: _____ Date: _____

 **Using a calculator, write each rational number as a repeating decimal.
Use bar notation to indicate the repeating digits.**

13. $\frac{18}{11}$ **14.** $\frac{5}{18}$

15. $\frac{17}{36}$ **16.** $\frac{29}{27}$

**Compare the positive rational numbers using the symbols < or >.
Use a number line to help you.**

┌─── *Example* ──┐

$\frac{9}{8}$ and $\frac{10}{9}$

$\frac{9}{8} = 1.125$

$\frac{10}{9} = 1.111... = 1.\overline{1}$

Write each rational number as a decimal.

Compare the decimals, __1.125__ and __1.$\overline{1}$__ .

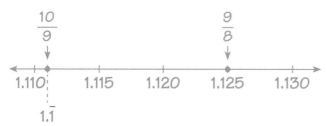

1.125 lies to the right of 1.$\overline{1}$ or 1.125 > 1.$\overline{1}$.

So, $\frac{9}{8} > \frac{10}{9}$.

└──┘

Name: _____   Date: _____

Complete.

17. $\frac{22}{7}$ and $\frac{25}{8}$

Write each rational number as a decimal.

$\frac{22}{7}$ = _____

$\frac{25}{8}$ = _____

Compare the decimals, _____ and _____.

Complete the number line and compare the numbers.

_____ lies to the right of _____

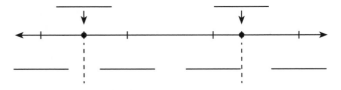

or _____ > _____.

So, _____ > _____.

Compare the positive rational numbers using the symbols < or >.
Use a number line to help you.

18. $\frac{3}{4}$ and $\frac{5}{6}$

19. $\frac{10}{11}$ and $\frac{9}{10}$

20. $\frac{13}{11}$ and $\frac{9}{8}$

21. $1\frac{7}{8}$ and $1\frac{8}{9}$

Compare the negative rational numbers using the symbols < or >.
Use a number line to help you.

Example

$-\dfrac{1}{4}$ and $-\dfrac{1}{5}$

Method 1
Compare using a number line.

$-\dfrac{1}{4} = -0.25$ Write each rational
number as a decimal.

$-\dfrac{1}{5} = -0.2$

$|-0.25| = 0.25$

$|-0.2| = 0.2$

Use the absolute value of −0.25 and −0.2 to help you graph the decimals on a number line.

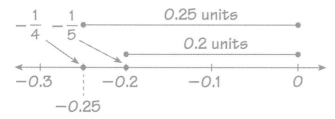

From the number line, you see that __−0.25__ lies farther to the left of 0 than __−0.2__
or $-0.2 > -0.25$.

So, $-\dfrac{1}{5} > -\dfrac{1}{4}$.

Method 2
Compare using place value. Write an inequality using the
absolute value of the two numbers.

$|-0.25| > |-0.2|$

The two numbers are negative, so the number with the greater
absolute value is farther to the left of 0. It is the lesser number.

$-0.2 > -0.25$

$-\dfrac{1}{5} > -\dfrac{1}{4}$

Complete.

22. $-2\frac{7}{8}$ and $-2\frac{8}{9}$

Method 1
Compare using a number line.

$-2\frac{7}{8} = $ _____

|_____| = _____

$-2\frac{8}{9} = $ _____ = _____

|_____| = _____

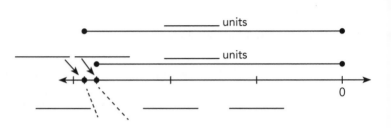

From the number line, you see that _____ lies farther to the left

of 0 than _____ or _____ > _____.

So, _____ > _____.

Method 2
Compare using place value.

|_____| < |_____|

The number with the greater absolute value is _____ and it is farther to the

left of 0. Hence it is the _____ number, or _____ > _____.

So, _____ > _____.

Compare the negative rational numbers using the symbols < or >.
Use a number line to help you.

23. $-\frac{3}{4}$ and $-\frac{4}{5}$

24. $-\frac{22}{7}$ and $-3\frac{1}{10}$

Name: _____   Date: _____

Lesson 1.3   Introducing Irrational Numbers

Circle all the irrational numbers in each set of numbers.

1. $\sqrt{4}, 5, \frac{1}{9}, \sqrt{2}, -2.31, \sqrt{7}$

2. $-\frac{19}{11}, -\sqrt{23}, 13, \sqrt{8}, 3.001$

Locate each positive irrational number on the number line using rational approximation.

Example

$\sqrt{13}$

$\sqrt{13}$ should lie between 3 and 4 because $3^2 = 9$ and $4^2 = 16$.

Step 1
Find an approximate value for $\sqrt{13}$ by using a calculator: $\sqrt{13}$ = __3.605551275...__

$\sqrt{13}$ lies between the tenths __3.6__ and __3.7__. So, $3.6 < \sqrt{13} < 3.7$.

Step 2
Graph the interval from 3.6 to 3.7 on a number line.

3.6   3.7

Step 3
The value of $\sqrt{13}$ with two decimal places is __3.61__.

3.61 is closer to __3.6__ than to __3.7__. So, $\sqrt{13}$ is located closer to __3.6__.

Step 4
Use 3.61 to locate $\sqrt{13}$ approximately
on the number line.

3.6   3.7
$\sqrt{13}$

Complete.

3. $\sqrt{14}$

Which two whole numbers is $\sqrt{14}$ between? _____ and _____

Find an approximate value of $\sqrt{14}$ by using a calculator: $\sqrt{14}$ = _____

$\sqrt{14}$ lies between the tenths _____ and _____.

The value of $\sqrt{14}$ with 2 decimal places is _____.

Which tenth is $\sqrt{14}$ located closer to? _____.

Name: _____ Date: _____

Locate each positive irrational number on the number line using rational approximations. First tell which two whole numbers the square root is between.

4. $\sqrt{8}$

5. $\sqrt{6}$

6. $\sqrt{23}$

7. $\sqrt{32}$

Locate each negative irrational number on the number line using rational approximations. First tell which two integers the square root is between.

--- Example ---

$-\sqrt{11}$

Because $3^2 = 9$ and $4^2 = 16$, $\sqrt{11}$ is between 3 and 4, and $-\sqrt{11}$ is between -3 and -4.

Step 1
Find an approximate value for $-\sqrt{11}$ by using a calculator: $-\sqrt{11} = \underline{-3.31662479...}$

$-\sqrt{11}$ lies between the tenths $\underline{-3.3}$ and $\underline{-3.4}$. So, $\underline{-3.4 < -\sqrt{11} < -3.3}$.

Step 2
Graph the interval from -3.3 to -3.4 on a number line.

Step 3
Use the approximate value of $-\sqrt{11}$ with 2 decimal places.

The value of $-\sqrt{11}$ with 2 decimal places is $\underline{-3.32}$.

-3.32 is closer to $\underline{-3.3}$ than to $\underline{-3.4}$. So, $-\sqrt{11}$ is located closer to $\underline{-3.3}$.

Step 4
Use -3.32 to locate $-\sqrt{11}$ approximately on the number line.

Name: _____   Date: _____

Complete.

8. $-\sqrt{8}$

Which two integers is $-\sqrt{8}$ between? _____ and _____

 Find an approximate value of $-\sqrt{8}$ by using a calculator: $-\sqrt{8}$ = _____

$-\sqrt{8}$ lies between the tenths _____ and _____.

The value of $-\sqrt{8}$ with 2 decimal places is _____.

Which tenth is $-\sqrt{8}$ closer to? _____

⟵——+—————————————————+———+——⟶

_____   _____ _____

Locate each negative irrational number on the number line using rational approximations. First tell which two integers the square root is between.

9. $-\sqrt{7}$

10. $-\sqrt{21}$

11. $-\sqrt{34}$

12. $-\sqrt{48}$

 Use a calculator. Locate each irrational number to 3 decimal places on the number line using rational approximations.

13. $\sqrt{53}$

14. $-\sqrt{117}$

Name: _____   Date: _____

Lesson 1.4 Introducing the Real Number System

 Using a calculator, compare each pair of real numbers using either < or >.

1. $\sqrt{11}$ ⬭ 3.32

2. $-\sqrt{7}$ ⬭ $-\sqrt{8}$

3. 20.182476 ⬭ 20.1824762...

4. -4.89898 ⬭ $-\sqrt{24}$

 Represent each real number as a decimal up to 3 decimal places. Locate each number on a real number line.

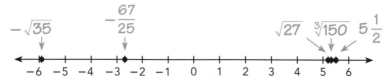

Example

$5\dfrac{1}{2}, \sqrt{27}, -\dfrac{67}{25}, -\sqrt{35}, \sqrt[3]{150}$

Use a calculator to represent each number in decimal form with 3 decimal places.

$5\dfrac{1}{2} = 5.500, \sqrt{27} \approx 5.196, -\dfrac{67}{25} = -2.680, -\sqrt{35} \approx -5.916, \sqrt[3]{150} \approx 5.313$

Ordering the numbers from the least to the greatest using the symbol <,

$-\sqrt{35} < -\dfrac{67}{25} < \sqrt{27} < \sqrt[3]{150} < 5\dfrac{1}{2}$

Locate each number approximately on the real number line.

```
        67
-√35    25              √27 ³√150 5 1/2
  ↓      ↓                ↘   ↓  ↙
←—+—●—+—+—●—+—+—+—+—+—+—|●●●—+—→
  -6 -5 -4 -3 -2 -1  0  1  2  3  4  5  6
```

Complete.

5. $0.\overline{831}, -\sqrt{8}, \dfrac{\pi}{2}, \dfrac{1}{7}, -\sqrt{7}$

Use a calculator to represent each number in decimal form with 3 decimal places.

$0.\overline{831} \approx$ _____, $-\sqrt{8} \approx$ _____, $\dfrac{\pi}{2} \approx$ _____, $\dfrac{1}{7} \approx$ _____, $-\sqrt{7} \approx$ _____

Ordering the numbers from least to greatest using the symbol <,

_____ < _____ < _____ < _____ < _____

Locate each number approximately
on the real number line.

```
←—+————+————+————+————+————+—→
 -3    -2    -1    0     1     2
```

Represent each real number as a decimal up to 3 decimal places. Locate each number on a real number line.

6. $\frac{10}{3}$, $\sqrt{10}$, $\frac{2\pi}{3}$, $\frac{3}{7}$, $\sqrt{3}$

7. $-\sqrt{7}$, $-\frac{11}{3}$, $0.\overline{54}$, $-\frac{\sqrt{5}}{2}$, $\frac{14}{15}$

8. $\frac{158}{60}$, $\sqrt{2}$, $\frac{\pi^2}{5}$, $\frac{3}{13}$, -0.84173

9. $-2.3\overline{84}$, $-\frac{4}{17}$, $-\sqrt{15}$, $-\frac{183}{58}$, $-\frac{\sqrt{99}}{8}$

Lesson 1.5 Introducing Significant Digits

List the significant digits for each number. Then write the number of significant digits.

> *Example*
>
> **a)** 0.050
>
>   <u>5 and 0</u> are significant digits.
>
>   There are ___2___ significant digits.
>
> **b)** 3.1402
>
>   <u>3, 1, 4, 0, and 2</u> are significant digits.
>
>   There are ___5___ significant digits.
>
> **c)** 0.001
>
>   ___1___ is a significant digit.
>
>   There is ___1___ significant digit.
>
> **d)** 10.0
>
>   <u>1, 0, and 0</u> are significant digits.
>
>   There are ___3___ significant digits.

Rule 1: All nonzero digits are significant.
Rule 2: Zeros in between nonzero digits are significant.
Rule 3: Trailing zeros in a decimal are significant.
Rule 4: Zeros on the left of the first nonzero digit are NOT significant.
Rule 5: Trailing zeros in an integer may or may not be significant due to rounding.

Complete.

1. 23.04

   _____ are significant digits.

   There are _____ significant digits.

2. 0.021

   _____ are significant digits.

   There are _____ significant digits.

3. 3,100

   _____ are significant digits.

   There are _____ significant digits.

4. 45.0

   _____ are significant digits.

   There are _____ significant digits.

5. 6.023

   _____ are significant digits.

   There are _____ significant digits.

6. 9,010

   _____ are significant digits.

   There are _____ significant digits.

Name: _____ Date: _____

Round each integer to the number of significant digits given.

┌─── *Example* ───┐
│   │
│ 5,379   (3 significant digits)   │
│   │
│ The 4th significant digit is ___9___, which is _greater than_ 5. │
│   │
│ 5,379 is closer to _5,380_ than to _5,370_.   │
│   │
│ So, the integer rounded to 3 significant digits is _5,380_. │
│   │
└───┘

Complete.

7. 128,043   (4 significant digits)

   The 5th significant digit is _____, which is _____ 5.

   128,043 is closer to _____ than to _____.

   So, the integer rounded to 4 significant digits is _____.

8. 150,659   (5 significant digits)

   The 6th significant digit is _____, which is _____ 5.

   150,659 is closer to _____ than to _____.

   So, the integer rounded to 5 significant digits is _____.

9. 23,513   (2 significant digits)

   The 3rd significant digit is _____.

   23,513 is exactly between _____ and _____.

   So, the integer rounded to 2 significant digits is _____.

Round each integer to the number of significant digits given.

10. 286   (2 significant digits)

11. 208,609   (4 significant digits)

12. 8,863   (3 significant digits)

13. 3,929,721   (6 significant digits)

Identify the significant digits in each number. Tell how many significant digits each number has.

Example

a) In 2009, the population of Willows, California was 6,300, rounded to the nearest 100.

<u>6 and 3</u> are significant digits. There are ___2___ significant digits.

b) The total length of the United States coastline is 89,600 miles, rounded to the nearest 100.

<u>8, 9, and 6</u> are significant digits. There are ___3___ significant digits.

c) The tallest mountain in California, Mount Whitney, stands at 14,510 feet, rounded to the nearest 10 feet.

<u>1, 4, 5, and 1</u> are significant digits. There are ___4___ significant digits.

Complete.

14. In 1690, the population of the United States was 210,400, rounded to the nearest 100.

_____ are significant digits. There are _____ significant digits.

15. The highest mountain in the United States is Mount McKinley, in Alaska. It stands 19,690 feet high, rounded to the nearest 10 feet.

_____ are significant digits. There are _____ significant digits.

16. California has a total length of about 8,300 miles of roadways, rounded to the nearest 100 miles.

_____ are significant digits. There are _____ significant digits.

Round each decimal to the number of significant digits given.

┌─── *Example* ───┐

0.02386   (2 significant digits)

Only 2 significant digits are required.

The 3rd significant digit is ____8____, which is __greater than__ 5.

So, the decimal rounded to 2 significant digits is __0.024__.

└───┘

Complete.

17. 19.6207   (4 significant digits)

Only 4 significant digits are required.

The 5th significant digit is _____, which is _____ 5.

So, the decimal rounded to 4 significant digits is _____.

18. 232.156   (5 significant digits)

Only 5 significant digits are required.

The 6th significant digit is _____, which is _____ 5.

So, the decimal rounded to 5 significant digits is _____.

19. 199.9995   (6 significant digits)

Only 6 significant digits are required.

The 7th significant digit is _____, which is _____ 5.

So, the decimal rounded to 6 significant digits is _____.

Round each decimal to the number of significant digits given.

20. 35.3719   (3 significant digits)

21. 6.02385   (5 significant digits)

22. 93.990096   (7 significant digits)

Name: _____   Date: _____

Use significant digits in a real-world situation.

┌─── *Example* ──┐

The length and width of a rectangle are 9.48 centimeters and 4.06 centimeters, as shown.

a) Calculate the area of the rectangle.

Area of rectangle = __9.48__ · __4.06__

= __38.4888__ cm²

The area of the rectangle is __38.4888__ square centimeters.

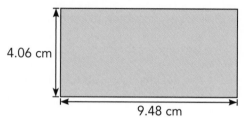
4.06 cm

9.48 cm

b) State the area of the rectangle correct to 3 significant digits.

The area of the rectangle correct to 3 significant digits is __38.5__ square centimeters.

└──┘

Complete.

23. A bag of marbles weighs 12.256 grams. Sam bought 8 such bags of marbles.

a) Calculate the total mass of the 8 bags of marbles.

Total mass = _____ · _____

= _____ g

b) State the total mass of the 8 bags correct to 2 significant digits.

_____ g

Solve.

24. The thickness of a stack of 15 identical plastic rulers is approximately 13.581 millimeters. What is the thickness of one plastic ruler correct to 3 significant digits?

Name: _____ Date: _____

CHAPTER

 Rational Number Operations

Lesson 2.1 Adding Integers

Complete each ☐ with > or <.

1. 22 ☐ −23

2. −13 ☐ −16

3. $-\frac{5}{7}$ ☐ $\frac{2}{7}$

4. −9.1 ☐ −8.3

Evaluate each expression.

5. $28 + (18 - 6) \cdot 5$

6. $4 \cdot (20 + 7) - 39$

Express each improper fraction as a mixed number.

7. $\frac{11}{8}$

8. $\frac{20}{6}$

Express each mixed number as an improper fraction.

9. $3\frac{2}{3}$

10. $5\frac{3}{7}$

Add or subtract. Express your answer in simplest form.

11. $\frac{3}{7} + \frac{1}{2}$

12. $3\frac{1}{6} - 1\frac{5}{9}$

Multiply or divide. Express your answer in simplest form.

13. $2\frac{1}{4} \cdot \frac{1}{3}$

14. $\frac{7}{9} \div \frac{28}{3}$

Multiply or divide.

15. $5.49 \div 0.6$

16. $5.4 \cdot 0.8$

Solve each percent problem.

17. 15% of $280

18. 110% of a number is 33. What is the number?

19. 14 bananas out of 70 fruits is what percent?

Solve.

20. James saved $580 in January. In February, he saved $1,044.

   a) Find the increase in his savings.

   b) Find the percent increase in his savings.

Add two negative integers.

Example

−3 + (−5)

Method 1

Use a number line to model the sum of two negative integers.

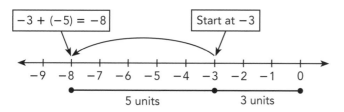

Start at −3. Then continue
by adding −5, a jump of
5 to the left to reach −8.

−3 + (−5) = ____−8____

Method 2

Use absolute values to find the sum of two negative integers.

$|-3| = 3$ Write the absolute value of each integer.
$|-5| = 5$
$|-3| + |-5| = 3 + 5$ Add the absolute values.
$= 8$ Simplify.
−3 + (−5) = ____−8____   Use the common sign, a negative sign, for the sum.

Complete.

21. −2 + (−1)

Method 1

Use a number line to model the sum of two negative integers.

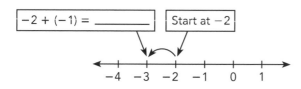

Start at −2. Then continue
by adding −1, a jump of
1 to the left to reach −3.

−2 + (−1) = _____

Method 2

Use absolute values to find the sum of two negative integers.

$|-2| =$ _____   Write the absolute value of each integer.

$|-1| =$ _____

$|-2| + |-1| =$ _____ + _____   Add the absolute values.

$=$ _____   Simplify.

$-2 + (-1) =$ _____   Use the common sign, a _____ sign, for the sum.

Evaluate each expression.

22. $-4 + (-5)$

23. $-11 + (-3)$

24. $-13 + (-5)$

25. $-8 + (-2)$

Add each integer and its opposite.

> **Example**
>
> $3 + (-3)$
>
>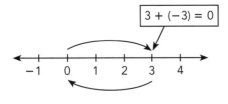
> $3 + (-3) = 0$
>
> Start at 0 and move 3 to the right of 0. Then add -3, a jump of 3 to the left.
>
> $3 + (-3) = \underline{\quad 0 \quad}$

26. $10 + (-10)$

27. $(-6) + 6$

Name: _____   Date: _____

Add two integers with different signs.

Example

−10 + 4

Method 1

Use a number line to model the sum of integers with different signs.

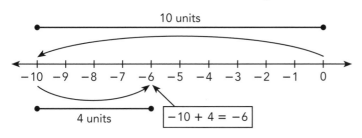

Start at 0 and move 10 to the left of 0. Then add 4, a jump of 4 to the right.

$$-10 + 4 = -6$$

OR

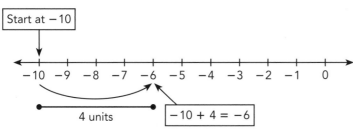

Start at −10. Then add 4, a jump of 4 to the right.

$$-10 + 4 = -6$$

−10 + 4 = ___−6___

Method 2

Use absolute values to find the sum of integers with different signs.

$$|-10| = 10$$ Write the absolute value of each integer.

$$|4| = 4$$

$$|-10| - |4| = 10 - 4$$ Subtract the lesser absolute value from the greater one.

$$= 6$$ Simplify.

$$-10 + 4 = \underline{-6}$$ Use a negative sign, because −10 has a greater absolute value.

Complete.

28. −14 + 8

$$|-14| = \underline{} \qquad |8| = \underline{}$$ Write the absolute value of each integer.

$$|-14| - |8| = \underline{} - \underline{}$$ Subtract the lesser absolute value from the greater one.

$$= \underline{}$$ Simplify.

$$-14 + 8 = \underline{}$$ Use a _____ sign, because _____ has a greater absolute value.

Evaluate the sum.

29. $-15 + 9$ **30.** $7 + (-18)$

Add more than two integers with different signs.

--- Example ---

$-7 + 1 + (-4)$

Method 1

Use a number line to model the sum of integers with different signs.

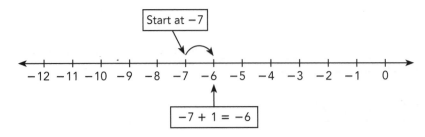

Start at -7. Then add 1, a jump of 1 to the right of -7.

$$-7 + 1 = -6$$

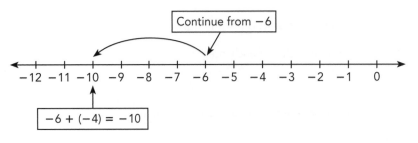

Continue by adding -4, a jump of 4 to the left of -6.

$$-6 + (-4) = -10$$

$$\text{So, } -7 + 1 + (-4) = -6 + (-4)$$
$$= -10$$

When you add more than two integers, you add any two integers at a time until you arrive at an answer. This is the associative property of addition.

You can also add 1 and -4 first. Then continue to add -7.
So, $-7 + 1 + (-4) = -7 + (-3)$
$= -10$

Method 2

Use absolute values to find the sum of integers with different signs.
First group integers with the same sign.

$-7 + 1 + (-4) = -7 + (-4) + 1$ Commutative property of addition

Next add -7 and -4.

> Moving from left to right, you can add any two integers that have the same sign. Add their absolute values and use the sign of the two integers for the sum.

$$|-7| = 7$$
$$|-4| = 4$$
     Write the absolute value of each integer.

$$|-7| + |-4| = 7 + 4$$
$$= 11$$
     Add the absolute values.
     Simplify.

$$-7 + (-4) = -11$$
     Use the common sign, a negative sign, for the sum.

Then continue by adding 1 to -11.

> You subtract the absolute values because the integers have different signs. Then use the sign of the greater absolute value for the sum.

$$|-11| = 11$$
$$|1| = 1$$
     Write the absolute value of each integer.

$$|-11| - |1| = 11 - 1$$
$$= 10$$
$$-11 + 1 = -10$$
     Subtract the lesser absolute value from the greater one.
     Simplify.
     Use a negative sign, because -11 has a greater absolute value.

$$So, -7 + 1 + (-4) = -7 + (-4) + 1$$
$$= -11 + 1$$
$$= -10$$

Complete.

31. $9 + (-5) + 8$

$9 + (-5) + 8 =$ _____ $+ 8$

$=$ _____

32. $-6 + 2 + (-8)$

$-6 + 2 + (-8) = -6 +$ _____ $+ 2$

$=$ _____ $+ 2$

$=$ _____

Evaluate each sum.

33. $-7 + (-8) + 10$

34. $4 + (-6) + (-3)$

Add integers with different signs in a real-world situation.

Example

The temperature in a town at 7 A.M. was −5°C. The temperature rose 7°C by noon and then fell 9°C by midnight. What was the temperature in the town at midnight?

> The verbal description can be translated as $-5 + 7 + (-9)$.

Method 1
Use a number line to model $-5 + 7 + (-9)$.

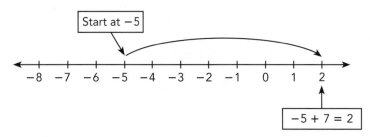

Start at −5.

$-5 + 7 = 2$

Start at −5. Then add 7, a jump of 7 to the right of −5.

$-5 + 7 = 2$

$2 + (-9) = -7$

Continue from 2

Continue by adding −9, a jump of 9 to the left of 2.

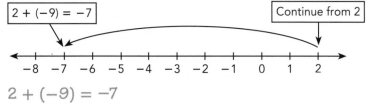

$2 + (-9) = -7$

So, $-5 + 7 + (-9) = 2 + (-9)$
$= -7$

The temperature in the town at midnight was __−7°C__.

Method 2

Use absolute values to evaluate $-5 + 7 + (-9)$.

First add -5 and 7.

$$|-5| = 5$$ Write the absolute value of each integer.
$$|7| = 7$$

$$|7| - |-5| = 7 - 5$$ Subtract the lesser absolute value from the greater one.
$$= 2$$ Simplify.
$$-5 + 7 = 2$$ Use a positive sign, because 7 has a greater absolute value.

Then add 2 and (-9).

$$|2| = 2$$ Write the absolute value of each integer.
$$|-9| = 9$$

$$|-9| - |2| = 9 - 2$$ Subtract the lesser absolute value from the greater one.
$$= 7$$ Simplify.
$$2 + (-9) = -7$$ Use a negative sign, because -9 has a greater absolute value.

$$\text{So, } -5 + 7 + (-9) = 2 + (-9)$$
$$= -7$$

The temperature in the town at midnight was __$-7°C$__.

Solve.

35. A helicopter rises 250 feet in the air, descends 150 feet, and then rises 97 feet. Overall, what is the distance the helicopter rises or falls?

Lesson 2.2   Subtracting Integers

Subtract positive integers.

> **Example**
>
> $12 - 15$
>
> $12 - 15 = 12 + (-15)$ Rewrite subtraction as adding the opposite.
>
> Using absolute values,
>
> $|-15| - |12| = 15 - 12$ Subtract the absolute values, because the addends have different signs.
> $\qquad\qquad = 3$ Simplify.
> $12 - 15 = 12 + (-15)$
> $\qquad\qquad = -3$ Use a negative sign, because -15 has a greater absolute value.

Complete.

1. A submarine is 250 feet below sea level. It descended 180 feet. How many feet below sea level is the submarine now?

   $-250 - 180 = -250 +$ _____   Rewrite subtraction as adding the opposite.

   Using absolute values,

   $|-250| + |\underline{\quad\quad}| = 250 +$ _____   Add the absolute values, because the addends have the same sign.

   $\qquad\qquad = $ _____   Simplify.

   $-250 - 180 = -250 + ($_____$)$

   $\qquad\qquad = $ _____   Use the common sign, a _____ sign, for the sum.

   The submarine is _____ feet below sea level now.

Evaluate each expression.

2. $18 - 32$

3. $15 - 27$

Name: _____   Date: _____

Solve.

4. The lowest temperature recorded in a particular state in January was −5°C.
   In February, the lowest temperature recorded was 16°C lower than the lowest
   temperature recorded in January. What was the lowest temperature recorded
   in February?

Subtract negative integers.

Example

a) $23 − (−6)$

   $23 − (−6) = 23 + 6$ Rewrite subtraction as adding the opposite.

   $\qquad\quad = 29$ Add.

b) $−12 − (−28)$

   $−12 − (−28) = −12 + 28$ Rewrite subtraction as adding the opposite.

   Using absolute values,

   $|−28| − |−12| = 28 − 12$ Subtract the absolute values.

   $\qquad\qquad = 16$ Simplify.

   $−12 − (−28) = −12 + 28$

   $\qquad\qquad = 16$ Use a positive sign, because −28 has a greater
                                absolute value.

Complete.

5. $22 − (−9)$

   $22 − (−9) = 22 +$ _____   Rewrite subtraction as adding the opposite.

   $\qquad = $ _____   Add.

Complete.

6. $-17 - (-5)$

$-17 - (-5) = -17 +$ _____   Rewrite subtraction as adding the opposite.

Using absolute values,

$|-17| - |-5| =$ _____ $-$ _____   Subtract the absolute values.

$=$ _____   Simplify.

$-17 - (-5) = -17 +$ _____

$=$ _____   Use a _____ sign, because _____ has a greater absolute value.

Evaluate each expression.

7. $17 - (-6)$

8. $-19 - (-11)$

Subtract negative integers.

Example

$-15 - (-7) - (-18)$

$\begin{aligned} -15 - (-7) - (-18) &= -15 + 7 + 18 \\ &= -8 + 18 \\ &= 10 \end{aligned}$ Rewrite subtraction as adding the opposite.
Add from left to right.
Simplify.

---

9. $-17 - (-5) - (-3)$

10. $-20 - (-15) - (-3)$

11. $-8 - (-18) - (-21)$

12. $-11 - (-19) - (-7)$

Name: _____   Date: _____

Find the distance between two integers.

> **Example**
>
> 5 and −7
>
> **Method 1**
> Use a number line to plot the points and count the units.
>
>
>
> 12 units
>
> The distance between 5 and −7 is ___12___ units.
>
> **Method 2**
> Use absolute value to find the distance between integers with different signs.
>
> Distance between 5 and −7:
>
> $|5-(-7)| = |5 + 7|$ Rewrite subtraction as adding the opposite.
>
> $= 12$ Add.

Complete.

13. Find the distance between 4 and −1.

  Method 1
  Use a number line to plot the points and count the units.

  The distance between 4 and −1 is _____ units.

  Method 2
  Use absolute values to find the distance between integers with opposite signs.

  Distance between 4 and −1:

  $|4 − (−1)| = |$_____$|$ Rewrite subtraction as adding the opposite.

  $=$ _____   Add.

Find the distance between the two integers.

14. −6 and 10

15. −19 and 7

Solve.

┌─── *Example* ───┐

The surface of the Salton Sea in California is 226 feet below sea level. The peak of Mount Whitney, also in California, is 14,505 feet above sea level. What is the difference between the two elevations?

Elevation of the Salton Sea: <u>−226 ft</u>
Elevation of Mount Whitney: <u>14,505 ft</u>
Difference between the two elevations:

$$|14{,}505 - (-226)| = |14{,}505 + 226|$$ Rewrite subtraction as adding the opposite.

$$= 14{,}731 \text{ ft}$$ Add.

The difference between the two elevations is <u>14,731</u> feet.

└──┘

Complete.

16. Jason and David went hiking at different times. Jason is currently 54 feet above sea level while David is just starting at 11 feet below sea level. What is the difference in their elevations?

Elevation of Jason: 54 ft   Elevation of David: _____ ft
Difference between their elevations:

$$|54 - (\text{_____})| = |\text{_____}|$$ Rewrite subtraction as adding the opposite.

$$= \text{_____ ft}$$ Add.

The difference in their elevations is _____ feet.

Solve.

17. Determine the difference in elevation between the summit of Arkansas' Magazine Mountain, 2,753 feet above sea level, and Death Valley, California, 282 feet below sea level.

Name: _____   Date: _____

Lesson 2.3 Multiplying and Dividing Integers

Evaluate each product.

> **Example**
>
> **a)** $-3 \cdot 5$
>
> $-3 \cdot 5 = 15$ Product of two integers with different signs is negative.
>
> **b)** $-2 \cdot (-6)$
>
> $-2 \cdot (-6) = 12$ Product of two integers with the same sign is positive.

1. $7 \cdot (-9)$

2. $4 \cdot (-9)$

3. $-4 \cdot (-7)$

4. $-5 \cdot (-5)$

Evaluate each product.

> **Example**
>
> $3 \cdot (-5) \cdot (-6)$
>
> **Method 1**
>
> $3 \cdot (-5) \cdot (-6) = (-15) \cdot (-6)$ Product of two integers with different signs is negative.
>
> $\qquad\qquad\qquad = 90$ Product of two integers with the same sign is positive.
>
> **Method 2**
>
> $3 \cdot (-5) \cdot (-6) = 3 \cdot (30)$ Product of two integers with the same sign is positive.
>
> $\qquad\qquad\qquad = 90$ Product of two integers with the same sign is positive.

5. $3 \cdot (-5) \cdot (-4)$

6. $5 \cdot (-7) \cdot (-2)$

Use multiplication in a real-world situation.

> *Example*
>
> The altitude of a hot air balloon was changing at a rate of –12 feet per second. Find the change in altitude of the hot air balloon after 6 seconds.
>
> Change in altitude = Rate · Time
>
> $\qquad\qquad = \underline{-12} \cdot \underline{6}$ Substitute –12 for rate and 6 for time.
>
> $\qquad\qquad = \underline{-72}$ ft   Multiply. Product of two integers with different signs is negative.
>
> The change in altitude of the hot air balloon is __–72__ feet.

Complete.

7. During an experiment, the temperature of a compound fell 2°C every minute. Find the total change in temperature of the compound after 9 minutes.

    Change in temperature = Rate · Time

    $\qquad\qquad = \underline{\hspace{2cm}} \cdot \underline{\hspace{2cm}}$ Substitute –2 for rate and 9 for time.

    $\qquad\qquad = \underline{\hspace{2cm}}$°C   Multiply. Product of two integers with different signs is negative.

    The total change in temperature of the compound is _____°C.

Solve.

8. In a quiz, points are awarded for each correct answer while points are deducted for each incorrect answer. In the first round, Ethan answered all the questions correctly. In the second round, he answered 8 questions incorrectly. If 3 points are deducted for each incorrect answer, by how much does Ethan's score change in the second round?

9. The elevators in the Empire State Building descend at a rate of about 7 meters per second. Find the change in altitude of an elevator that descends for 13 seconds.

Name: _____   Date: _____

Evaluate each quotient.

Example

a) $-27 \div (-3)$

$-27 \div (-3) = 9$ Divide. Quotient of two integers with the same sign is positive.

b) $-84 \div 7$

$-84 \div 7 = -12$ Divide. Quotient of two integers with different signs is negative.

c) $66 \div (-6)$

$66 \div (-6) = -11$ Divide. Quotient of two integers with different signs is negative.

---

10. $-40 \div (-5)$

11. $-36 \div 9$

12. $32 \div (-8)$

13. $-49 \div (-7)$

Solve.

14. In 200 seconds, a raindrop fell 5,000 feet to the ground. Find its change in height per second.

15. Find the change in height per second of a skydiver who falls 648 meters in 12 seconds.

Lesson 2.4 Operations with Integers

Apply the order of operations with integers.

Example

a) $-5 - 30 \div 5 - 15$

$-5 - 30 \div 5 - 15$

$= -5 - 6 - 15$ Divide.

$= -5 + (-6) + (-15)$ Rewrite subtraction as adding the opposite.

$= -5 + (-15) + (-6)$ Use commutative property of addition.

$= -20 + (-6)$ Add.

$= -26$ Add.

b) $-4 + (8 - 10) \cdot (-5)$

$-4 + (8 - 10) \cdot (-5)$

$= -4 + (-2) \cdot (-5)$ Simplify within the parentheses.

$= -4 + 10$ Multiply.

$= 6$ Add.

Complete.

1. $20 + 6 - 2 \cdot 4 = 20 + 6 -$ _____   Multiply.

$=$ _____ $+$ _____   Rewrite subtraction as adding the opposite.

$=$ _____   Add.

2. $(-15 - 25) \div 8 - 12 =$ _____ $\div 8 - 12$ Subtract within the parentheses.

$=$ _____ $- 12$ Divide.

$=$ _____   Subtract.

3. $-11 - (5 + 2) + 3 = -11 -$ _____ $+ 3$ Add within the parentheses.

$= -11 +$ _____ $+ 3$ Rewrite subtraction as adding the opposite.

$=$ _____ $+ 3$ Add.

$=$ _____   Add.

Evaluate each expression.

4. $-7 - 28 \div 4 - 13$

5. $-3 + (6 - 9) \cdot (-4)$

6. $(-35 - 5) \div 8 - 17$

7. $-13 - (4 + 4) \cdot 2$

Name: _____   Date: _____

Solve. Show your work.

Example

A rectangular piece of paper measuring 17 inches by 13 inches has four of its corners cut off as shown in the diagram. What is the remaining area?

Area of each square corner:
$3 \cdot 3 = 9 \text{ in}^2$

Area of remaining paper:
Area of original paper – Area of four cut-off squares
$= 17 \cdot 13 - (4 \cdot 9)$
$= 221 - 36$
$= 185 \text{ in}^2$

The area of the remaining paper is ___185___ square inches.

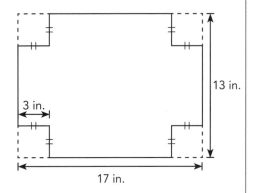

Complete.

8. A canteen operator paid $60 for 100 sandwiches. He sold two-fifths of them at $1 each and the rest at three for $2. What is his profit?

Two-fifth of 100: $(100 \div 5) \cdot 2 =$ _____ sandwiches

_____ sandwiches sold at $1 each: _____ · $1 = $_____

Number of sandwiches sold at three for $2: 100 – _____

                              = _____ sandwiches

Number of sets of _____ sandwiches: _____ ÷ 3 = _____ sets

Cost of _____ sets of sandwiches: _____ · $2 = $_____

Profit: $_____ + $_____ – $_____ = $_____

His profit is $_____.

Calculate the area of each figure.

9.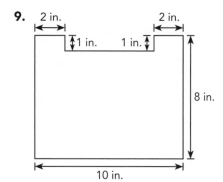

10.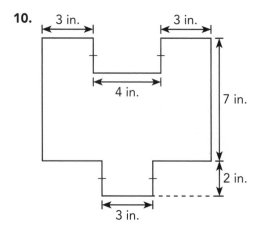

Solve. Show your work.

11. A shopkeeper paid $80 for 80 bagels. He sold half of them at $2 each and the rest at $1 each. What is his profit?

12. A shopkeeper paid $100 for 50 yogurt bars. He sold two-fifths of them at $3 each and the rest at $2 each. What is his profit?

Lesson 2.5 Operations with Rational Numbers

Add rational numbers.

> **Example**
>
> **a)** $\dfrac{-2}{3} + \dfrac{1}{-5}$
>
> $\dfrac{-2}{3} + \dfrac{1}{-5} = \dfrac{-2 \cdot (-5)}{3 \cdot (-5)} + \dfrac{1 \cdot 3}{-5 \cdot 3}$ Write as equivalent fractions using the LCD, -15.
>
> $\qquad\qquad = \dfrac{10}{-15} + \dfrac{3}{-15}$ Multiply all products.
>
> $\qquad\qquad = \dfrac{10 + 3}{-15}$ Simplify using a single denominator.
>
> $\qquad\qquad = \dfrac{13}{-15}$ Add.
>
> $\qquad\qquad = -\dfrac{13}{15}$ Write as equivalent fraction.
>
> **b)** $1\dfrac{2}{3} + \left(-2\dfrac{1}{4}\right)$
>
> $1\dfrac{2}{3} + \left(-2\dfrac{1}{4}\right) = 1 + \dfrac{2}{3} + (-2) + \left(-\dfrac{1}{4}\right)$ Rewrite the sum.
>
> $\qquad\qquad = 1 + (-2) + \left(\dfrac{2}{3}\right) + \left(-\dfrac{1}{4}\right)$ Use the commutative property of addition.
>
> $\qquad\qquad = -1 + \dfrac{2 \cdot 4}{3 \cdot 4} + \left(-\dfrac{1 \cdot 3}{4 \cdot 3}\right)$ Write equivalent fractions using the LCD, 12.
>
> $\qquad\qquad = -1 + \dfrac{8}{12} + \left(-\dfrac{3}{12}\right)$ Multiply all products.
>
> $\qquad\qquad = -1 + \dfrac{5}{12}$ Add the fractions.
>
> $\qquad\qquad = -\dfrac{12}{12} + \dfrac{5}{12}$ Write an equivalent fraction for the integer part.
>
> $\qquad\qquad = -\dfrac{7}{12}$ Add the like fractions.

c) $\dfrac{2}{3} + \left(\dfrac{-5}{8}\right) + \dfrac{1}{6}$

$\dfrac{2}{3} + \left(\dfrac{-5}{8}\right) + \dfrac{1}{6} = \dfrac{2 \cdot 8}{3 \cdot 8} + \dfrac{-5 \cdot 3}{8 \cdot 3} + \dfrac{1 \cdot 4}{6 \cdot 4}$ Write equivalent fractions using the LCD of all three fractions.

$= \dfrac{16}{24} + \left(\dfrac{-15}{24}\right) + \dfrac{4}{24}$ Multiply all products.

$= \dfrac{16 + (-15) + 4}{24}$ Rewrite using single denominator.

$= \dfrac{5}{24}$ Add.

Complete.

1. $-1\dfrac{1}{2} + 2\dfrac{3}{8}$

$-1\dfrac{1}{2} + 2\dfrac{3}{8} = -1 \underline{\hspace{2cm}} + 2 \underline{\hspace{2cm}}$ Rewrite the fraction part of each mixed number using the LCD.

$= (-1 + 2) - \underline{\hspace{2cm}} + \underline{\hspace{2cm}}$ Use the commutative property of addition to group the integers and then the fractions.

$= \underline{\hspace{2cm}} + \underline{\hspace{2cm}}$ Add.

$= \underline{\hspace{2cm}}$ Write as a mixed number.

2. $\dfrac{1}{4} + \left(\dfrac{-5}{12}\right) + \left(\dfrac{-2}{3}\right)$

$\dfrac{1}{4} + \left(\dfrac{-5}{12}\right) + \left(\dfrac{-2}{3}\right) = \underline{\hspace{2cm}} + \underline{\hspace{2cm}} + \underline{\hspace{2cm}}$ Write equivalent fractions using the LCD.

$= \underline{\hspace{3cm}}$ Multiply all products.

$= \underline{\hspace{2cm}}$ Write using a single denominator.

$= \underline{\hspace{2cm}}$ Add.

$= \underline{\hspace{2cm}}$ Write in simplest form.

Evaluate each expression.

3. $\frac{-3}{4} + \left(\frac{1}{-5}\right)$

4. $-1\frac{1}{3} + 2\frac{5}{6}$

5. $\frac{1}{3} + \left(\frac{-5}{6}\right) + \left(\frac{-3}{4}\right)$

6. $\frac{2}{3} + \left(\frac{-3}{8}\right) - \frac{1}{4}$

Subtract rational numbers.

Example

a) $2\frac{3}{4} - 5\frac{1}{3}$

$$2\frac{3}{4} - 5\frac{1}{3} = 2\frac{3 \cdot 3}{4 \cdot 3} - 5\frac{1 \cdot 4}{3 \cdot 4}$$
Write equivalent fractions for the fraction part of each mixed number using the LCD, 12.

$$= 2\frac{9}{12} - 5\frac{4}{12}$$
Multiply all products.

$$= 2 + \frac{9}{12} - 5 - \frac{4}{12}$$
Rewrite the sum.

$$= 2 - 5 + \left(\frac{9}{12} - \frac{4}{12}\right)$$
Use the commutative property of addition.

$$= -3 + \frac{5}{12}$$
Add the integers and fractions.

$$= -2\frac{7}{12}$$
Simplify.

b) $\frac{1}{4} - \frac{3}{8} - \frac{1}{16}$

$$\frac{1}{4} - \frac{3}{8} - \frac{1}{16} = \frac{1 \cdot 4}{4 \cdot 4} - \frac{3 \cdot 2}{8 \cdot 2} - \frac{1}{16}$$
Write equivalent fractions using the LCD for all three fractions, 16.

$$= \frac{4}{16} - \frac{6}{16} - \frac{1}{16}$$
Multiply all products.

$$= \frac{4 - 6 - 1}{16}$$
Rewrite using a single denominator.

$$= -\frac{3}{16}$$
Subtract.

Name: _____   Date: _____

Complete.

7. $\dfrac{1}{5} - \dfrac{2}{15}$

$\dfrac{1}{5} - \dfrac{2}{15} = \dfrac{1 \cdot 3}{5 \cdot 3} - \dfrac{2}{15}$ Write equivalent fractions using the LCD.

$= \underline{\hspace{1.5cm}} - \dfrac{2}{15}$ Multiply all products.

$= \underline{\hspace{1.5cm}}$ Subtract.

8. $2\dfrac{1}{3} - 5\dfrac{4}{9}$

$2\dfrac{1}{3} - 5\dfrac{4}{9} = 2 + \underline{\hspace{1.5cm}} - 5 - \underline{\hspace{1.5cm}}$ Rewrite mixed number as integers and fractions.

$= 2 - 5 + \underline{\hspace{1.5cm}} - \underline{\hspace{1.5cm}}$ Rewrite as equivalent fraction.

$= -3 + \underline{\hspace{1.5cm}} - \underline{\hspace{1.5cm}}$

$= -3 + \underline{\hspace{1.5cm}}$

$= \underline{\hspace{1.5cm}}$

9. $\dfrac{3}{18} - \dfrac{5}{6} - \dfrac{2}{9}$

$\dfrac{3}{18} - \dfrac{5}{6} - \dfrac{2}{9} = \dfrac{3}{18} - \dfrac{5 \cdot 3}{6 \cdot 3} - \dfrac{2 \cdot 2}{9 \cdot 2}$ Write equivalent fractions using the LCD.

$= \dfrac{3}{18} - \underline{\hspace{1.5cm}} - \underline{\hspace{1.5cm}}$ Multiply all products.

$= \underline{\hspace{1.5cm}}$ Rewrite using a single denominator.

$= \underline{\hspace{1.5cm}}$ Add.

$= \underline{\hspace{1.5cm}}$ Simplify.

Evaluate each expression.

10. $2\dfrac{2}{3} - 4\dfrac{1}{4}$

11. $\dfrac{1}{8} - \dfrac{5}{24} - \dfrac{7}{12}$

Name: _____   Date: _____

Subtract rational numbers in a real-world situation.

Example

Mrs. June has a roll of string $22\frac{1}{3}$ feet long. She needs $25\frac{5}{6}$ feet to tie up a parcel. How much more string does she need?

$22\frac{1}{3} - 25\frac{5}{6}$ Write an expression for this situation.

$= 22\frac{1 \cdot 2}{3 \cdot 2} - 25\frac{5}{6}$ Write equivalent fractions for the fraction parts using the LCD, 6.

$= 22\frac{2}{6} - 25\frac{5}{6}$ Multiply all products.

$= 22 + \frac{2}{6} - 25 - \frac{5}{6}$ Rewrite the sum.

$= 22 - 25 + \left(\frac{2}{6} - \frac{5}{6}\right)$ Use the commutative property of addition to group the integers and then the fractions.

$= -3 + \left(-\frac{3}{6}\right)$ Subtract the integers and then the fractions.

$= -3\frac{3}{6}$ Subtract.

$= -3\frac{1}{2}$ Write in the simplest form.

She needs ___$3\frac{1}{2}$___ feet of string.

Solve.

12. A storm in Florida collected $14\frac{4}{5}$ inches of rainwater in northeast Palm Bay, Florida and $12\frac{1}{10}$ inches of rainwater in northwest of Palm Shores. What is the difference in rainfall over the two locations?

   a) Write a subtraction expression for the difference in depth of these two recorded rainfalls.

   b) Find the difference in these two recorded rainfalls.

Solve.

13. A plank of wood has an original length of $10\frac{1}{2}$ feet. $3\frac{3}{8}$ feet is sawn off. What is the remaining length of wood?

14. The world's largest chicken egg has a length of $3\frac{11}{12}$ inches as compared to the average length of $2\frac{3}{4}$ inches. What is the difference in length?

15. The world's tallest man stands at $8\frac{1}{12}$ feet while the shortest man stands at $2\frac{5}{12}$ feet. What is the difference in their heights?

Multiply rational numbers.

Example

a) $\frac{-3}{5} \cdot \frac{25}{12}$

$\frac{-3}{5} \cdot \frac{25}{12} = \frac{-3 \cdot 25}{5 \cdot 12}$ Multiply the numerators, and multiply the denominators.

$= \frac{-{}^1\cancel{3} \cdot \cancel{25}^5}{\cancel{5}_1 \cdot \cancel{12}_4}$ Divide the numerator and denominator by their greatest common factor (GCF).

$= -\frac{5}{4}$ Simplify.

$= -1\frac{1}{4}$ Write as a mixed number.

---

b) $-1\frac{3}{5} \cdot 4\frac{3}{8}$

$$-1\frac{3}{5} \cdot 4\frac{3}{8} = -\frac{8}{5} \cdot \frac{35}{8}$$ Write as improper fractions.

$$= \frac{-{}^1\cancel{8} \cdot \cancel{35}^7}{{}_1\cancel{5} \cdot \cancel{8}_1}$$ Divide the numerator and denominator by their GCF.

$$= \frac{-7}{1}$$ Simplify.

$$= -7$$ Write as a negative integer.

Complete.

16. $-\frac{3}{7} \cdot \frac{7}{12}$

$-\frac{3}{7} \cdot \frac{7}{12} =$ _____   Multiply the numerators, and multiply the denominators.

$=$ _____   Divide the numerator and denominator by their GCF.

$=$ _____   Simplify.

17. $\left(-3\frac{2}{3}\right) \cdot 2\frac{2}{5}$

$\left(-3\frac{2}{3}\right) \cdot 2\frac{2}{5} = -\dfrac{\boxed{}}{3} \cdot \dfrac{\boxed{}}{5}$ Write as improper fractions.

$=$ _____   Divide the numerator and denominator by their GCF.

$=$ _____   Simplify.

$=$ _____   Write as a mixed number.

Evaluate each expression.

18. $-\frac{2}{9} \cdot \frac{27}{28}$

19. $-2\frac{2}{15} \cdot \left(-3\frac{3}{8}\right)$

Divide rational numbers.

┌─ *Example* ──

a) $-\dfrac{4}{5} \div \dfrac{8}{15}$

$-\dfrac{4}{5} \div \dfrac{8}{15} = -\dfrac{4}{5} \cdot \dfrac{15}{8}$ Multiply $-\dfrac{4}{5}$ by the reciprocal of $\dfrac{8}{15}$.

$\qquad\qquad = \dfrac{-4 \cdot 15}{5 \cdot 8}$ Multiply the numerators and denominators.

$\qquad\qquad = \dfrac{-\,^1\!\!\!\!4 \cdot 15^{\,3}}{\,_1 5 \cdot 8_{\,2}}$ Divide the numerator and denominator by the GCF.

$\qquad\qquad = -\dfrac{3}{2}$ Simplify.

$\qquad\qquad = -1\dfrac{1}{2}$ Write as a mixed number.

b) $\left(-3\dfrac{1}{5}\right) \div \left(4\dfrac{4}{15}\right)$

$\left(-3\dfrac{1}{5}\right) \div \left(4\dfrac{4}{15}\right) = \left(-\dfrac{16}{5}\right) \div \left(\dfrac{64}{15}\right)$ Write as improper fractions.

$\qquad\qquad = -\dfrac{16}{5} \cdot \dfrac{15}{64}$ Multiply $-\dfrac{16}{5}$ by the reciprocal of $\dfrac{64}{15}$.

$\qquad\qquad = \dfrac{-16 \cdot 15}{5 \cdot 64}$ Multiply the numerators and denominators.

$\qquad\qquad = \dfrac{-\,^1\!\!\!\!16 \cdot 15^{\,3}}{\,_1 5 \cdot 64_{\,4}}$ Divide the numerator and denominator by the GCF.

$\qquad\qquad = -\dfrac{3}{4}$ Simplify.

c) $\dfrac{-\left(\dfrac{1}{2}\right)}{\left(\dfrac{1}{8}\right)}$

$\dfrac{-\left(\dfrac{1}{2}\right)}{\left(\dfrac{1}{8}\right)} = -\dfrac{1}{2} \div \dfrac{1}{8}$ Rewrite as a division expression.

$\qquad\quad = -\dfrac{1}{2} \cdot \dfrac{8}{1}$ Multiply $\dfrac{1}{2}$ by the reciprocal of $\dfrac{1}{8}$.

$\qquad\quad = -\dfrac{8}{2}$ Multiply the numerators and denominators.

$\qquad\quad = -4$ Simplify.

└───

Complete.

20. $\dfrac{9}{20} \div \left(-\dfrac{3}{35}\right)$

$\dfrac{9}{20} \div \left(-\dfrac{3}{35}\right) = \dfrac{9}{20} \cdot \left(-\dfrac{\boxed{}}{3}\right)$ Multiply $\dfrac{9}{20}$ by the reciprocal of $\dfrac{3}{35}$.

$\qquad\qquad = \underline{\hspace{2cm}}$ Divide the numerators and denominators by the GCF.

$\qquad\qquad = \underline{\hspace{2cm}}$ Simplify.

$\qquad\qquad = \underline{\hspace{2cm}}$ Write as a mixed number.

21. $\dfrac{\left(\dfrac{1}{2}\right)}{\left(-\dfrac{3}{10}\right)}$

$\dfrac{\left(\dfrac{1}{2}\right)}{\left(-\dfrac{3}{10}\right)} = \dfrac{1}{2} \div \left(-\dfrac{3}{10}\right)$ Rewrite as a division expression.

$\qquad\qquad = \dfrac{1}{2} \cdot \left(-\dfrac{10}{\boxed{}}\right)$ Multiply $\dfrac{1}{2}$ by the reciprocal of $\dfrac{3}{10}$.

$\qquad\qquad = \underline{\hspace{2cm}}$ Divide the numerators and denominators by the GCF.

$\qquad\qquad = \underline{\hspace{2cm}}$ Simplify.

$\qquad\qquad = \underline{\hspace{2cm}}$ Write as a mixed number.

Evaluate each expression.

22. $\dfrac{7}{20} \div \left(-\dfrac{14}{15}\right)$

23. $-4\dfrac{1}{6} \div \left(1\dfrac{1}{9}\right)$

24. $\dfrac{\left(\dfrac{1}{3}\right)}{\left(-\dfrac{2}{9}\right)}$

25. $-\dfrac{7}{11} \div \dfrac{7}{22}$

Lesson 2.6 Operations with Decimals

Add and subtract decimals.

> **Example**
>
> **a)** $-5.21 + 2.49$
>
> Using absolute values,
>
> $|-5.21| - |2.49| = 5.21 - 2.49$ Subtract the lesser absolute value from the greater one.
>
> $\qquad\qquad\qquad = 2.72$ Simplify.
>
> $-5.21 + 2.49 = -2.72$ Use a negative sign, because -5.21 has a greater absolute value.
>
> **b)** $-2.34 - 6.21$
>
> $-2.34 - 6.21 = -2.34 + (-6.21)$ Rewrite as adding the opposite.
>
> Using absolute values,
>
> $|-2.34| + |-6.21| = 2.34 + 6.21$ Add the absolute values.
>
> $\qquad\qquad\qquad = 8.55$ Simplify.
>
> $-2.34 - 6.21 = -8.55$ Use the common sign, a negative sign.

Complete.

1. $3.62 + (-4.09)$

Using absolute values,

_____ − _____ = _____ − _____   Subtract the lesser absolute value from the greater absolute value.

$\qquad\qquad\quad = $ _____   Simplify.

$3.62 + (-4.09) = $ _____   Use a _____ sign, because _____ has a greater absolute value.

Evaluate.

2. $-3.53 + 5.27$ **3.** $-2.05 - 3.65$

Name: _____ Date: _____

Add and subtract decimals in a real-world situation.

Example

The water level in a pond was 4.21 feet. During a heavy downpour, it rose by 1.19 feet, but in summer the water level dropped by 2.32 feet. What is the final water level?

$4.21 + 1.19 - 2.32$ Write an expression.

$= 5.4 - 2.32$ Subtract.

$= 3.08$ Simplify

The final water level is __3.08__ feet.

Complete.

4. At noon, the temperature was 70.5°F. By midnight, the temperature dropped by 10.9°F. The next morning, the temperature rose by 12.1°F. What is the final temperature?

$70.5 -$ _____ $+$ _____   Write an expression.

$=$ _____ $+$ _____   Add.

$=$ _____   Simplify.

The final temperature is _____°F.

Solve.

5. A water tank has a water level of 8.5 feet. Due to a leak, the water level fell by 2.21 feet. The tank was then repaired and more water was pumped into it. The water level rose by 3.27 feet. What is the new water level?

6. At noon, the temperature was 6.9°F. By midnight, the temperature dropped by 8.5°F. The next morning, it fell further by 2.3°F. What is the final temperature?

Multiply decimals.

Example

a) $-6.83 \cdot (-0.4)$

$$
\begin{array}{r}
^{3}6.{}^{1}8\,3 \leftarrow \\
\times \quad 0.4 \leftarrow \\
\hline
2\,7\,3\,2 \\
0\,0\,0 \\
\hline
2.7\,3\,2 \leftarrow \\
\end{array}
$$

2 decimal places
+ 1 decimal place

Multiply the numbers without their signs.

3 decimal places   Add.

$$-6.83 \cdot (-0.4) = 2.732$$

Product of two decimals with different signs is negative.

b) $-4.3 \cdot (-1.5)$

$$
\begin{array}{r}
^{1}4.3 \leftarrow \\
\times \ 1.5 \leftarrow \\
\hline
2\,1\,5 \\
4\,3 \\
\hline
6.45 \leftarrow \\
\end{array}
$$

1 decimal place
+ 1 decimal place

Multiply the numbers without their signs.

2 decimal places   Add.

$$-4.3 \cdot (-1.5) = 6.45$$

Product of two decimals with the same sign is positive.

c) 7% of $890

$$
\begin{array}{r}
^{6}8\,9\,0 \leftarrow \\
\times \ \ 0.0\,7 \leftarrow \\
\hline
6\,2\,3\,0 \\
0\,0\,0 \\
0\,0\,0 \\
\hline
0\,6\,2.3\,0 \leftarrow \\
\end{array}
$$

0 decimal place
+ 2 decimal places

Multiply the numbers without their signs.

2 decimal places   Add.

$$7\% \text{ of } \$890 = \$62.30$$

Product of two decimals with the same sign is positive.

Name: _____   Date: _____

Complete.

7. 19.3 · (−0.6)

$^{5}1^{9}$9.3
×   0.6   Multiply the numbers without their signs.

――――――   Add.

19.3 · (−0.6) = _____   Product of two decimals with different signs is negative.

Evaluate each product.

8. 5.39 · (−0.6)

9. (−5.3) · (−2.8)

10. (−22.9) · (3.1)

11. 4% of $19

Divide a decimal by a decimal.

> **Example**
>
> **a)** 16.68 ÷ (−1.2)
>
>
>
> $\quad\quad\begin{array}{r} 13.9 \\ 12\overline{)166.8} \\ 12 \\ \hline 46 \\ 36 \\ \hline 108 \\ 108 \\ \hline 0 \end{array}$
>
> Place the decimal point in the quotient above the decimal point in the dividend.
>
> Make the divisor a whole number by multiplying both the divisor and the dividend by 10.
>
> You use a negative sign because the two decimals have different signs.
>
> 16.68 ÷ (−1.2) = −13.9

Complete.

12. $(-23.49) \div 0.9$

$(-23.49) \div 0.9 = $ _____ $\div 9$

$= $ _____

Evaluate each quotient.

13. $11.36 \div (-1.6)$

14. $5.49 \div (-6.1)$

15. $-73.53 \div (0.9)$

16. $(-54.96) \div (1.2)$

Apply the order of operations to decimals.

> *Example*
>
> **a)** A hot air balloon rose 5.5 feet per second for 15 seconds. It then descended at 2.3 feet per second for 8 seconds. What is the overall change in altitude?
>
> $(5.5 \cdot 15) - (2.3 \cdot 8) = 82.5 - 18.4$ Multiply.
>
> $= 64.1$ Subtract.
>
> The overall change in altitude is __64.1__ feet.
>
> **b)** A baseball jacket costs $60 plus 4% tax. What is the total cost of the jacket?
>
> **Method 1**
>
> $\$60 + 0.04 \cdot \$60 = \$60 + \$2.40$ Multiply.
>
> $= \$62.40$ Add.
>
> The total cost of the jacket is __$62.40__.
>
> **Method 2**
>
> $\$60 \cdot 1.04 = \$62.40$ Multiply.
>
> The total cost of the jacket is __$62.40__.

Complete.

17. A hot air balloon rose 4.5 feet for 20 seconds and then descended at 2.1 feet
per second for 10 seconds. What is the overall change in altitude?

$(4.5 \cdot$ _____$) - ($_____ $\cdot 10) = $ _____ $-$ _____   Multiply.

$=$ _____   Subtract.

The overall change in altitude is _____ feet.

18. A tennis racket costs $58 plus 4% tax. How much does the racket cost?

Method 1

$58 + ($_____ $\cdot \$$_____$) = \$58 + \$$_____   Multiply.

$= \$$_____   Add.

The cost of the tennis racket is $_____.

Method 2

$58 \cdot$ _____ $= \$$_____   Multiply.

The cost of the tennis racket is $ _____.

Solve.

19. A diver at 20.5 feet below sea level dives further down at 1.5 feet per second
for 15 seconds. How deep is he below sea level?

20. A baseball cap costs $18 plus 5% tax. How much does the cap cost?

Name: _____   Date: _____

Apply the order of operations to decimals.

Example

James bought some shares in a business. In a month, the value of each share rose from $1.08 to $1.18. What is the percent change? Round your answer to the nearest hundredth of a percent.

Percent change:

$$\frac{(1.18 - 1.08)}{1.08} \cdot 100\% = \frac{0.1}{1.08} \cdot 100\% \qquad \text{Subtract.}$$

$$\approx 9.26\% \qquad \text{Simplify.}$$

The percent change in the value

of each share is about __9.26%__.

> If there is a drop in the value of the share, the percent change is negative.

Complete.

21. Over a five year period, the population of a city changed from 2.4 million to 1.92 million. What was the percent change in the city's population?

Percent change: $\dfrac{\boxed{} - \boxed{}}{2.4} \cdot 100\%$

$= \underline{\hspace{2cm}} \cdot 100\%$

$= \underline{\hspace{2cm}}$

The percent change in the city's population is _____%.

Solve. Round your answer to the nearest hundredth of a percent.

22. Over a decade, the population of Michigan changed from 2.4 million to 9.883 million. What is the percent change?

23. Over a decade, the population of Utah grew from 2.23 million to 2.76 million. What is the percent change?

CHAPTER

Algebraic Expressions

Lesson 3.1 Adding Algebraic Terms

Consider the algebraic expression $2x + 5$. State the following.

1. How many terms are there? _____

2. State the coefficient of the algebraic term. _____

3. What is the constant term? _____

4. Write the operation symbol. _____

Evaluate each expression by replacing all its variables with their assigned values.

5.

x	$x + 7$	$5x$	$3x - 1$
-1			
0			
-2			
5			

Simplify each expression where possible.

6. $x + y - 3$

7. $4g - 2g$

8. $3n + 7n + 2$

9. $4p - 3p + 5p$

Expand each expression.

10. $3(x + 2)$

11. $5(2 + 3m)$

12. $2(4y - 7)$

13. $7(4 - 3p)$

Factor each expression.

14. $2n + 6$

15. $6x + 9$

16. $10p - 5$

17. $12 - 15y$

Choose an equivalent expression.

18. $9m - 12$ is equivalent to _____.
   a) $4(3m - 3)$

   c) $9(m - 3)$

   b) $3(3m - 4)$

   d) $12(m - 1)$

***x* is an unknown number. Write an expression for each of the following.**

19. 3 less than the number _____

20. Product of 7 and the number _____

21. 2 more than twice the number _____

22. 8 less than one-third of the number _____

Simplify the algebraic expression with decimal coefficients by adding.

--- Example ---

$0.8x + 0.6x$

| 0.8x | 0.6x |

0.1x

x

From the bar model,

$0.8x + 0.6x =$ ___1.4x___

Represent the term 0.8x with eight 0.1x sections and the term 0.6x with six 0.1x sections. The sum is the total number of shaded sections in the model.

Complete.

23. $0.3y + 0.4y$

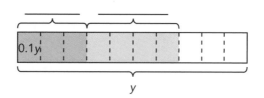

From the bar model,

$0.3y + 0.4y = $ _____

Simplify each expression with decimal coefficients.

24. $0.1m + 0.3m$

25. $0.4h + 0.9h$

26. $0.3x + 0.7x$

27. $0.9g + 0.8g$

Simplify the algebraic expression with fractional coefficients by adding.

> *Example*
>
> $x + \dfrac{2}{2}x$
>
> **Method 1**
> Use a bar model.
>
>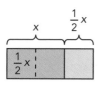
>
> From the bar model,
>
> $x + \dfrac{2}{2}x = \underline{\dfrac{3}{2}x}$
>
> **Method 2**
> Use a common denominator for both coefficients.
>
> $x + \dfrac{2}{2}x = \underline{\dfrac{\frac{2}{2}x}{}} + \underline{\dfrac{\frac{1}{2}x}{}}$
>
> $= \underline{\dfrac{\frac{3}{2}x}{}}$
>
> Rewrite x as $\dfrac{2}{2}x$.
>
> The coefficient is greater than 1. Leave it as an improper fraction.
>
>

Name: _____   Date: _____

Complete.

28. $x + \frac{1}{3}x$

Method 1
Use a bar model.

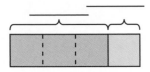

From the bar model,

$x + \frac{1}{3}x = $ _____

Method 2
Rewrite the coefficients.

$x + \frac{1}{3}x = $ _____ $+ \frac{1}{3}x$

$= $ _____

Simplify each expression with fractional coefficients.

29. $x + \frac{1}{5}x$

30. $b + \frac{2}{7}b$

Simplify the algebraic expression with fractional coefficients by adding.

> **Example**
>
> $\frac{1}{4}x + \frac{1}{3}x$
>
> **Method 1**
> Use a bar model.
>
> $\frac{1}{4}x = \frac{3}{12}x$ $\frac{1}{3}x = \frac{4}{12}x$
>
> $\frac{1}{12}x$
>
> x
>
> From the bar model,
>
> $\frac{1}{4}x + \frac{1}{3}x = \dfrac{\frac{7}{12}x}{}$
>
> **Method 2**
> Rewrite the coefficients.
>
> $\frac{1}{4}x + \frac{1}{3}x = \dfrac{\frac{3}{12}x + \frac{4}{12}x}{}$
>
> $= \dfrac{\frac{7}{12}x}{}$
>
>
>
> The LCM of the denominators 3 and 4 is 12.

Name: _____ Date: _____

Complete.

31. $\frac{1}{3}x + \frac{1}{6}x$

Method 1
Use a bar model.

$\frac{1}{3}x = $ _____ _____

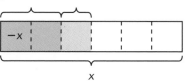

From the bar model,

$\frac{1}{3}x + \frac{1}{6}x = $ _____

$= $ _____

Method 2
Rewrite the coefficients.

$\frac{1}{3}x + \frac{1}{6}x = $ _____ + _____

$= $ _____

$= $ _____

Simplify each expression with fractional coefficients.

32. $\frac{1}{2}p + \frac{1}{3}p$

33. $\frac{1}{2}d + \frac{3}{10}d$

34. $\frac{2}{3}k + \frac{3}{5}k$

35. $\frac{3}{4}y + \frac{1}{6}y$

36. $\frac{4}{5}a + \frac{2}{6}a$

37. $\frac{2}{9}w + \frac{1}{2}w$

Lesson 3.2 Subtracting Algebraic Terms

Simplify the algebraic expression with decimal coefficients by subtracting.

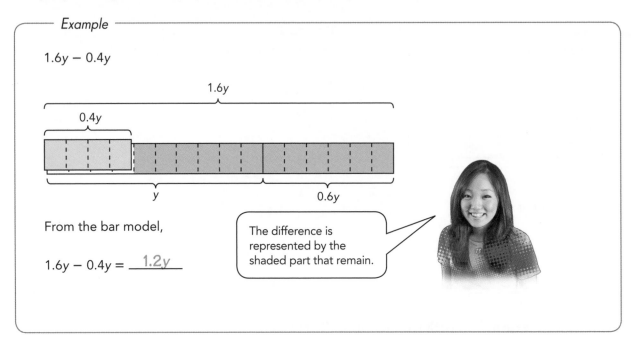

Example

$1.6y - 0.4y$

1.6y

0.4y

y

0.6y

From the bar model,

The difference is represented by the shaded part that remain.

$1.6y - 0.4y =$ ___1.2y___

Complete.

1. $0.8b - 0.3b$

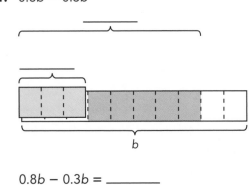

b

$0.8b - 0.3b =$ _____

Simplify each expression with decimal coefficients.

2. $1.3a - 0.5a$

3. $4.7g - 0.6g$

4. $0.9h - 0.5h$

5. $1.8p - 1.3p$

Name: _____ Date: _____

Simplify the algebraic expression with fractional coefficients by subtracting.

Example

$\frac{5}{8}x - \frac{1}{4}x$

Method 1
Use a bar model.

From the bar model,

$\frac{5}{8}x - \frac{1}{4}x = \underline{\frac{3}{8}x}$

Method 2
Rewrite the coefficients.

$\frac{5}{8}x - \frac{1}{4}x = \underline{\frac{5}{8}x - \frac{2}{8}x}$

$= \underline{\frac{3}{8}x}$

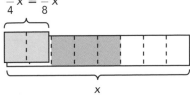

$\frac{5}{8}x$

$\frac{1}{4}x = \frac{2}{8}x$

x

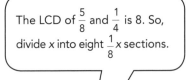

The LCD of $\frac{5}{8}$ and $\frac{1}{4}$ is 8. So, divide x into eight $\frac{1}{8}x$ sections.

The LCD of $\frac{5}{8}$ and $\frac{1}{4}$ is 8.

Rewrite the coefficients as fractions with denominator 8.

Complete.

6. $\frac{5}{6}x - \frac{2}{3}x$

Method 1
Use a bar model.

$\frac{5}{6}x$

$\frac{2}{3}x = \underline{\hspace{2cm}}$

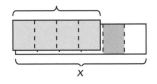

x

From the bar model,

$\frac{5}{6}x - \frac{2}{3}x = \underline{\hspace{2cm}}$

Method 2
Rewrite the coefficients.

$\frac{5}{6}x - \frac{2}{3}x = \underline{\hspace{1.5cm}} - \underline{\hspace{1.5cm}}$

$= \underline{\hspace{1.5cm}}$

Complete.

7. $\frac{5}{4}p - \frac{1}{2}p$

Method 1
Use a bar model.

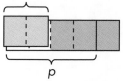

$$\frac{1}{2}p = \underline{\hspace{2cm}}$$

From the bar model,

$$\frac{5}{4}p - \frac{1}{2}p = \underline{\hspace{2cm}}$$

Method 2
Rewrite the coefficients.

$$\frac{5}{4}p - \frac{1}{2}p = \underline{\hspace{2cm}} - \underline{\hspace{2cm}}$$

$$= \underline{\hspace{2cm}}$$

Simplify each expression with fractional coefficients.

8. $\frac{1}{2}x - \frac{1}{8}x$

9. $\frac{7}{9}y - \frac{1}{6}y$

10. $\frac{5}{6}m - \frac{3}{4}m$

11. $\frac{7}{8}d - \frac{2}{3}d$

12. $\frac{11}{8}k - \frac{3}{4}k$

13. $\frac{6}{5}w - \frac{1}{2}w$

Lesson 3.3 Simplifying Algebraic Expressions

Simplify the algebraic expression with more than two terms and involving decimal coefficients.

> **Example**
>
> $0.5p + 0.9p + 2$
>
> From the bar model,
> $0.5p + 0.9p + 2$
>
> $= \underline{1.4p + 2}$
>
>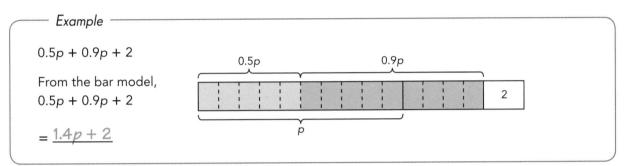

Complete to simplify each expression.

1. $1.3x + 3x + 4$

   $\underbrace{1.3x + 3x} + 4$

   $= \underline{\hspace{1.5cm}} + \underline{\hspace{1.5cm}}$

2. $1.7y - 0.8y - 3$

   $\underbrace{1.7y - 0.8y} - 3$

   $= \underline{\hspace{1.5cm}} - \underline{\hspace{1.5cm}}$

Simplify each expression with one variable.

3. $3.4f - 1.3f + 5$

4. $0.6g + 1.9g - 2$

Simplify the algebraic expression with more than two terms and involving fractional coefficients.

> **Example**
>
> $\frac{3}{4}x + \frac{1}{8}x + 3 - 2$
>
> $\frac{3}{4}x + \frac{1}{8}x + 3 - 2 = \underbrace{\frac{6}{8}x + \frac{1}{8}x} + \underbrace{3 - 2}$ The LCD of $\frac{3}{4}$ and $\frac{1}{8}$ is 8. Rewrite the coefficients
> as fractions with denominator 8.
>
> $= \underline{\frac{7}{8}x} + \underline{1}$

Complete.

5. $\dfrac{3}{5}y - \dfrac{3}{10}y - 1 + 3$

$\dfrac{3}{5}y - \dfrac{3}{10}y - 1 + 3$

$= \underline{\hspace{1.5cm}} - \dfrac{3}{10}y - 1 + 3$

$= \underline{\hspace{1.5cm}} + \underline{\hspace{1.5cm}}$

6. $\dfrac{2}{3}d - \dfrac{1}{4}d - 2 - 5$

$\dfrac{2}{3}d - \dfrac{1}{4}d - 2 - 5$

$= \underline{\hspace{1.5cm}} - \underline{\hspace{1.5cm}} - 2 - 5$

$= \underline{\hspace{1.5cm}} - \underline{\hspace{1.5cm}}$

Simplify algebraic expressions with three like terms.

> *Example*
>
> **a)** $0.9w + 0.3w + 0.5w$
>
> $0.9w + 0.3w + 0.5w = \underline{\;\;1.2w\;\;} + 0.5w$ Add the first two like terms.
>
> $= \underline{\;\;1.7w\;\;}$ Simplify.
>
> **b)** $\dfrac{1}{4}b + \dfrac{3}{4}b - \dfrac{1}{8}b$
>
> $\dfrac{1}{4}b + \dfrac{3}{4}b - \dfrac{1}{8}b = \underline{\;\;1b\;\;} - \dfrac{1}{8}b$ Add the first two like terms.
>
> $= \underline{\;\;\dfrac{8}{8}b\;\;} - \underline{\;\;\dfrac{1}{8}b\;\;}$ Rewrite the coefficients to have a common denominator 8.
>
> $= \underline{\;\;\dfrac{7}{8}b\;\;}$ Subtract the two like terms.

Complete.

7. $1.6x + 0.5x - 0.8x$

$1.6x + 0.5x - 0.8x$

$= \underline{\hspace{1.5cm}} - 0.8x$

$= \underline{\hspace{1.5cm}}$

8. $\dfrac{2}{7}y + \dfrac{1}{14}y + \dfrac{5}{7}y$

$\dfrac{2}{7}y + \dfrac{1}{14}y + \dfrac{5}{7}y$

$= \underline{\hspace{1.5cm}} + \dfrac{1}{14}y + \underline{\hspace{1.5cm}}$

$= \underline{\hspace{1.5cm}} + \underline{\hspace{1.5cm}}$

$= \underline{\hspace{1.5cm}}$

Simplify each expression with three algebraic terms.

9. $3.5m - 2.1m + 0.9m$

10. $4.2g + 1.7g - 2.4g$

11. $\frac{3}{8}s + \frac{1}{8}s + \frac{1}{6}s$

12. $\frac{1}{4}c + \frac{1}{3}c - \frac{5}{12}c$

Simplify algebraic expressions by grouping like terms.

> *Example*
>
> **a)** $6k + 8 - 4k + 3$
>
> $6k + 8 - 4k + 3 = \underline{\quad 6k \quad} - \underline{\quad 4k \quad} + 8 + 3$ Group like terms.
>
> $= \underline{\quad 2k \quad} + \underline{\quad 11 \quad}$ Simplify.
>
> **b)** $\frac{3}{5}d + \frac{3}{7} + \frac{1}{5}d - \frac{1}{7}$
>
> $\frac{3}{5}d + \frac{3}{7} + \frac{1}{5}d - \frac{1}{7} = \underline{\quad \frac{3}{5}d \quad} + \underline{\quad \frac{1}{5}d \quad} + \underline{\quad \frac{3}{7} \quad} - \underline{\quad \frac{1}{7} \quad}$ Group like terms.
>
> $= \underline{\quad \frac{4}{5}d \quad} + \underline{\quad \frac{2}{7} \quad}$ Simplify.

Complete.

13. $6b + 4 + 7b + 9$

$6b + 4 + 7b + 9$

$= \underline{\qquad} + \underline{\qquad} + 4 + 9$

$= \underline{\qquad} + \underline{\qquad}$

14. $\frac{4}{9}d + \frac{2}{7} - \frac{2}{9}d - \frac{1}{7}$

$\frac{4}{9}d + \frac{2}{7} - \frac{2}{9}d - \frac{1}{7}$

$= \underline{\qquad} - \underline{\qquad} + \underline{\qquad} - \underline{\qquad}$

$= \underline{\qquad} + \underline{\qquad}$

Simplify each expression by grouping like terms.

15. $9n + 1 - 3n - 4$

16. $\frac{4}{7}f - \frac{3}{7} + \frac{1}{7}f + \frac{5}{7}$

Simplify algebraic expressions with two variables.

Example

a) $2y + 5x + 4y + 9x$

$2y + 5x + 4y + 9x = (\underline{2y} + \underline{4y}) + (\underline{5x} + \underline{9x})$ Group like terms.

$= \underline{6y} + \underline{14x}$ Simplify.

b) $6a - 3b - a + 7b$

$6a - 3b - a + 7b = (\underline{6a} - \underline{a}) + (\underline{7b} - \underline{3b})$ Group like terms.

$= \underline{5a} + \underline{4b}$ Simplify.

Complete.

17. $8d + 9w + d + 8w$

$8d + 9w + d + 8w$

$= (\underline{} + \underline{}) + (\underline{} + \underline{})$ Group like terms.

$= \underline{} + \underline{}$ Simplify.

Simplify each expression with two variables.

18. $3a - b + 4b + 6a$

19. $7x - 3y - 3x + 5y$

20. $9g - 5h + 4g + 9h$

21. $p - 9r + 3p + 3r$

Name: _____ Date: _____

Lesson 3.4 Expanding Algebraic Expressions

Expand the algebraic expression with fractional factors.

Example

$\frac{1}{3}(6x + 12)$

Method 1
Use a bar model.

Arrange the bar model for 6x + 12 into 3 equal groups to find one third of (6x + 12).

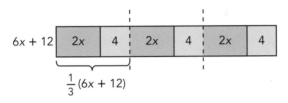

$6x + 12$ | 2x | 4 | 2x | 4 | 2x | 4 |

$\frac{1}{3}(6x + 12)$

From the bar model,

$\frac{1}{3}(6x + 12) = \underline{\quad 2x \quad} + \underline{\quad 4 \quad}$

Method 2
Use the distributive property.

$\frac{1}{3}(6x + 12) = \frac{1}{3}(\underline{\ 6x\ }) + \frac{1}{3}(\underline{\ 12\ })$ Use the distributive property.

$\qquad\qquad = \underline{\quad 2x \quad} + \underline{\quad 4 \quad}$ Multiply.

Complete.

1. $\frac{1}{2}(4x + 6)$

Method 1
Use a bar model.

$4x + 6$ | 2x | 3 | 2x | 3 |

$\frac{1}{2}(4x + 6)$

From the bar model,

$\frac{1}{2}(4x + 6) = \underline{\qquad} + \underline{\qquad}$

Method 2
Use the distributive property.

$\frac{1}{2}(4x + 6) = \frac{1}{2}(\underline{\qquad}) + \frac{1}{2}(\underline{\qquad})$

$\qquad\qquad = \underline{\qquad} + \underline{\qquad}$

Name: _____   Date: _____

Expand each expression with fractional factors.

2. $\frac{1}{4}(12x + 16)$

3. $\frac{1}{5}(10x + 35)$

4. $\frac{1}{3}(8m + 6)$

5. $\frac{1}{8}(7 + 3n)$

Expand the algebraic expression with decimal factors.

Example

$0.6(0.3x - 5)$

$0.6(0.3x - 5) = 0.6[0.3x + (-5)]$ Rewrite subtraction as adding the opposite.

$= 0.6(\underline{0.3x}) + 0.6(\underline{-5})$ Use the distributive property.

$= \underline{0.18x} + (\underline{-3})$ Multiply.

$= \underline{0.18x} - \underline{3}$ Rewrite the expression.

6. $0.3(3x + 7)$

$0.3(3x + 7)$

$= 0.3(\underline{\hspace{1cm}}) + 0.3(\underline{\hspace{1cm}})$

$= \underline{\hspace{1cm}} + \underline{\hspace{1cm}}$

7. $0.9(2.1y - 2)$

8. $1.5(0.4p + 2.1)$

9. $1.3(3w - 1.1)$

Expand algebraic expressions with negative factors.

Example

a) $-2\left(\dfrac{1}{4}a + \dfrac{1}{8}\right)$

$-2\left(\dfrac{1}{4}a + \dfrac{1}{8}\right) = -2 \underline{\quad \left(\dfrac{1}{4}a\right) \quad} + (-2)\underline{\quad \left(\dfrac{1}{8}\right) \quad}$ Use the distributive property.

$= \underline{\quad -\dfrac{1}{2}a \quad} + \underline{\quad \left(-\dfrac{1}{4}\right) \quad}$ Multiply.

$= \underline{\quad -\dfrac{1}{2}a \quad} - \underline{\quad \dfrac{1}{4} \quad}$ Rewrite the expression.

b) $-\dfrac{1}{3}(-2x + 6y)$

$-\dfrac{1}{3}(-2x + 6y) = -\dfrac{1}{3}\underline{\quad (-2x) \quad} + \left(-\dfrac{1}{3}\right)\underline{\quad (6y) \quad}$ Use the distributive property.

$= \underline{\quad \dfrac{2}{3}x \quad} + \underline{\quad (-2y) \quad}$ Multiply.

$= \underline{\quad \dfrac{2}{3}x \quad} - \underline{\quad 2y \quad}$ Rewrite the expression.

c) $-(2.5m - 3.6)$

$-(2.5m - 3.6) = -1[\underline{\quad 2.5m \quad} + (\underline{\quad -3.6 \quad})]$ Rewrite the expression.

$= -1(\underline{\quad 2.5m \quad}) + (-1)(\underline{\quad -3.6 \quad})$ Use the distributive property.

$= \underline{\quad -2.5m \quad} + \underline{\quad 3.6 \quad}$ Multiply.

Complete.

10. $-3(-5a - 6)$

$= -3[-5a + (\underline{\hspace{1.5cm}})]$

$= -3(\underline{\hspace{1.5cm}}) + (-3)(\underline{\hspace{1.5cm}})$

$= \underline{\hspace{1.5cm}}$

11. $-\frac{1}{4}(4y + 7)$

$= -\frac{1}{4}(\underline{\hspace{1.5cm}}) + \left(-\frac{1}{4}\right)(\underline{\hspace{1.5cm}})$

$= \underline{\hspace{1.5cm}} + \underline{\hspace{1.5cm}}$

$= \underline{\hspace{1.5cm}}$

Expand each expression with negative factors.

12. $-3\left(2x + \frac{1}{3}\right)$

13. $-5\left(\frac{3}{10}a - 2\right)$

14. $-\frac{1}{2}\left(-4x + \frac{1}{3}\right)$

15. $-0.6(-7x - 9)$

Expand and simplify the algebraic expression.

> **Example**
>
> $3(a + 2b) - 4b$
>
> $3(a + 2b) - 4b = 3(\underline{\quad a \quad}) + 3(\underline{\quad 2b \quad}) - \underline{\quad 4b \quad}$ Use the distributive property.
>
> $= \underline{\quad 3a \quad} + \underline{\quad 6b \quad} - \underline{\quad 4b \quad}$ Multiply.
>
> $= \underline{\quad 3a \quad} + \underline{\quad 2b \quad}$ Simplify.

Complete.

16. $4(2d + 3f) + 6d = 4(2d) + 4(\underline{\hspace{1.5cm}}) + \underline{\hspace{1.5cm}}$ Use the distributive property.

$= \underline{\hspace{1.5cm}} + \underline{\hspace{1.5cm}} + \underline{\hspace{1.5cm}}$ Multiply.

$= \underline{\hspace{1.5cm}} + \underline{\hspace{1.5cm}} + \underline{\hspace{1.5cm}}$ Group like terms.

$= \underline{\hspace{1.5cm}} + \underline{\hspace{1.5cm}}$ Simplify.

Expand and simplify each expression.

17. $4(g + 5h) + 3h$

18. $6x + 3(7y + x)$

Expand and simplify the expression.

> *Example*
>
> $-3\left(\dfrac{2}{3}x - 2\right) + 4x$
>
> $-3\left(\dfrac{2}{3}x - 2\right) + 4x = -3[\underline{\dfrac{2}{3}x} + (\underline{-2})] + \underline{4x}$ Rewrite the expression.
>
> $\qquad = -3 \ \underline{\left(\dfrac{2}{3}x\right)} + (-3)(\underline{-2}) + \underline{4x}$ Use the distributive property.
>
> $\qquad = \underline{-2x} + \underline{6} + \underline{4x}$ Multiply.
>
> $\qquad = \underline{-2x} + \underline{4x} + \underline{6}$ Group like terms.
>
> $\qquad = \underline{2x} + \underline{6}$ Simplify.

Complete.

19. $-2(1.5y - 1) - 2y$

$\qquad -2(1.5y - 1) - 2y = -2[1.5y + (\underline{\hspace{1.5cm}})] - 2y$ Rewrite the expression.

$\qquad\qquad = -2(\underline{\hspace{1.2cm}}) + (-2)(\underline{\hspace{1.2cm}}) - \underline{\hspace{1.2cm}}$ Use the distributive property.

$\qquad\qquad = \underline{\hspace{1.2cm}} + \underline{\hspace{1.2cm}} - \underline{\hspace{1.2cm}}$ Multiply.

$\qquad\qquad = \underline{\hspace{1.2cm}} - \underline{\hspace{1.2cm}} + \underline{\hspace{1.2cm}}$ Group like terms.

$\qquad\qquad = \underline{\hspace{1.2cm}} + \underline{\hspace{1.2cm}}$ Simplify.

Expand and simplify each expression.

20. $-4\left(\dfrac{1}{4}g - 2\right) - 3g$

21. $-4(1.5m - 3) + 6m$

Name: _____ Date: _____

Expand and simplify the expression.

> **Example**
>
> $2(3a + 1) - (b + 2)$
>
> $2(3a + 1) - (b + 2)$
>
> $= 2(\underline{3a + 1}) + (\underline{-1})(\underline{b + 2})$ Rewrite the expression.
>
> $= 2(\underline{\;3a\;}) + 2(\underline{\;1\;}) + (-1)(\underline{\;b\;}) + (-1)(\underline{\;2\;})$ Use the distributive property.
>
> $= \underline{\;6a\;} + \underline{\;2\;} + \underline{\;(-b)\;} + \underline{\;(-2)\;}$ Multiply.
>
> $= \underline{\;6a\;} + \underline{\;(-b)\;} + \underline{\;2\;} + \underline{\;(-2)\;}$ Group like terms.
>
> $= \underline{\;6a\;} - \underline{\;b\;}$ Remove parentheses and simplify.

Complete.

22. $3(2a + 4) - 2(b - 2)$

$3(2a + 4) - 2(b - 2)$

$= 3(2a + 4) + (\underline{\quad})(\underline{\quad} - \underline{\quad})$ Rewrite the expression.

$= 3(\underline{\quad}) + 3(\underline{\quad}) + (\underline{\quad})(\underline{\quad}) + (\underline{\quad})(\underline{\quad})$ Use the distributive property.

$= \underline{\quad} + \underline{\quad} + \underline{\quad} + \underline{\quad}$ Multiply.

$= \underline{\quad} + \underline{\quad} + \underline{\quad} + \underline{\quad}$ Group like terms.

$= \underline{\qquad\qquad}$ Remove parentheses and simplify.

Expand and simplify the expression.

23. $4\left(\dfrac{1}{2}x - 3\right) - (y + 4)$ **24.** $-2(m - 4) - 2(2n - 2)$

25. $3(d + 7) - 2(3g - 2)$ **26.** $-6(p - 3) - (5q - 4)$

Lesson 3.5 Factoring Algebraic Expressions

Factor the algebraic expression with two variables.

Example

$2x - 6y$

Method 1
Use a bar model.

$2x - 6y$ | x | x | −y | −y | −y | −y | −y | −y |

Draw a group of two x sections and six −y sections.

$2x - 6y$
| x | −y | −y | −y |
| x | −y | −y | −y |

Rearrange into two identical groups. Each group has one x section and three −y sections.

From the bar model,

$2x - 6y = \underline{2(x - 3y)}$

Method 2
Use the distributive property.

$2x - 6y = 2x + (\underline{-6y})$ Rewrite the expression.

$= \underline{2}(\underline{x}) + \underline{2}(\underline{-3y})$ The GCF of 2x and −6y is 2.

$= \underline{2}(\underline{x - 3y})$ Factor 2 from each term.

Complete.

1. $3a - 15b$

$3a - 15b = \underline{\hspace{2cm}} + (\underline{\hspace{2cm}})$ Rewrite the expression.

$= \underline{\hspace{1.5cm}}(\underline{\hspace{1.5cm}}) + \underline{\hspace{1.5cm}}(\underline{\hspace{1.5cm}})$ The GCF of 3a and −15b is _____.

$= \underline{\hspace{1.5cm}}(\underline{\hspace{1.5cm}})$ Factor _____ from each term.

Factor each expression with two variables.

2. $3x - 12y$ **3.** $7m - 21n$

Factor algebraic expressions with negative terms.

Example

a) $-5x - 2$

$$-5x - 2 = -5x + (\underline{-2})$$ Rewrite the expression.

$$= \underline{-1}(\underline{5x}) + (\underline{-1})(\underline{2})$$ The GCF of $-5x$ and -2 is (-1).

$$= \underline{-1}(\underline{5x + 2})$$ Factor (-1) from each term.

$$= -\underline{(5x + 2)}$$ Simplify.

b) $-3b - 6$

$$-3b - 6 = -3b + (\underline{-6})$$ Rewrite the expression.

$$= \underline{-3}(\underline{b}) + (\underline{-3})(\underline{2})$$ The GCF of $-3b$ and -6 is (-3).

$$= \underline{-3}(\underline{b + 2})$$ Factor (-3) from each term and simplify.

Complete.

4. $-4x - 7$

$$-4x - 7 = -4x + (\underline{})$$ Rewrite the expression.

$$= \underline{}(\underline{}) + (\underline{})(\underline{})$$ The GCF of $-4x$ and -7 is $(\underline{})$.

$$= \underline{}(\underline{})$$ Factor $(\underline{})$ from each term.

$$= \underline{}$$ Simplify.

5. $-8a - 12b$

$$-8a - 12b = \underline{} + (\underline{})$$ Rewrite the expression.

$$= \underline{}(\underline{}) + (\underline{})(\underline{})$$ The GCF of $-8a$ and $-12b$ is $(\underline{})$.

$$= \underline{}(\underline{})$$ Factor $(\underline{})$ from each term and simplify.

Factor each expression with negative terms.

6. $-3x - 1$

7. $-5 - 4m$

8. $-6a - 9b$

9. $-4m - 12n$

Name: _____   Date: _____

Lesson 3.6 Writing Algebraic Expressions

Translate each verbal description into an algebraic expression.
Simplify the expression where possible.

> *Example*
>
> **a)** Last week, a painter mixed x quarts of white paint with some red paint to make 12 quarts of pink paint. This week, he uses 20% less white paint to make the pink paint. Write an expression for the number of quarts of pink paint he made this week.
>
> $\underline{12}$ plus $\underline{-0.2}$ times $\underline{x}$
>
> $\underline{\quad -0.2 \quad} \cdot \quad x$ Translate by parts.
>
> $12 \quad + \quad \underline{\quad -0.2x \quad}$ Combine.
>
> $12 + (-0.2x) = 12 - 0.2x$
>
> ($\underline{\quad 12 - 0.2x \quad}$) quarts of pink paint were made this week.
>
>
>
> $20\% = \dfrac{20}{100}$
> $= 0.2$
>
> **b)** In January, Sarah deposited y dollars in the bank. At the end of the year, she received 2% interest. Write an expression for the amount of money she had in her bank account at the end of the year.
>
> $\underline{y}$ increased by $\underline{2\%}$
>
> $\qquad\qquad$ 2% of y
>
> $\qquad\qquad = $
>
> $y \qquad + \qquad \underline{\quad 0.02y \quad}$ Translate by parts.
>
> $\underline{\quad y + 0.02y \quad}$ Combine.
>
> $= \underline{\quad 1.02y \quad}$ Simplify.
>
> She had $\underline{\;1.02y\;}$ dollars in her bank account at the end of the year.
>
> **c)** Five jugs each contained q liters of water. Mark needs one-third of the amount of water less 5 liters. Find the amount of water Mark needs.
>
> $\underline{\text{One-third}}$ of the $\underline{\text{product of 5 and } q}$ less $\underline{5}$
>
> $\dfrac{1}{3} \qquad\qquad \cdot \qquad\qquad 5q \qquad - \qquad 5$
>
> $\dfrac{5}{3}q \qquad\qquad\qquad - \qquad 5$
>
> $\dfrac{5}{3}q - 5$
>
> Mark needs $\dfrac{5}{3}q - 5$ liters of water.

Complete.

1. Paige purchased 5x pounds of flour to make 4 identical sponge cakes. How much flour does each sponge cake require?

   5x   shared among   4

   _____   ÷   4

   = _____

   Each sponge cake requires _____ pounds of flour.

2. David bought an antique watch for w dollars. He later sold it and made a 30% profit. Write an algebraic expression for the sales price of the watch.

   w   increased by   30%

   _____% of w

   =

   w   +   _____w

   _____ + _____

   = _____

   He sold the watch for _____ dollars.

**Translate the verbal description into an algebraic expression.
Simplify the expression where possible.**

3. Gary earned x dollars and James earned $\frac{1}{3}x$ dollars last month. Gary saved half of his income and James saved one-fifth of his income. Write an expression for the total amount that Gary and James saved.

Name: _____   Date: _____

Solve. You may use a diagram, model, or table.

Example

a) The length of a basketball court is $(8x - 10)$ feet and its width is $6x$ feet. Write an algebraic expression for the perimeter of the court.

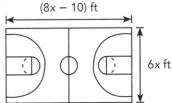

Perimeter of the field:

$(8x - 10) + 6x + (8x - 10) + 6x = 28x - 20$

The perimeter of the court is $(\underline{28x - 20})$ feet.

b) At a supermarket, cherry tomatoes are sold for $0.75 per pound, zucchinis are sold for $1.80 per pound, and red peppers are sold for $3.45 per pound. Danny bought x pounds of cherry tomatoes, $\frac{1}{2}x$ pounds of zucchinis, and $3y$ pounds of red peppers. What was the total cost of the vegetables purchased by Danny?

Vegetable	Price Per Pound	Total Weight	Cost
Cherry Tomatoes	$0.75	x pounds	0.75x dollars
Zucchinis	$1.80	$\frac{1}{2}x$ pounds	0.90x dollars
Red Peppers	$3.45	$3y$ pounds	10.35y dollars

Total cost of vegetables:

$0.75x + 0.90x + 10.35y = 1.65x + 10.35y$

The total cost of the vegetables was $(\underline{1.65x + 10.35y})$ dollars.

c) Sandy had m balloons, but then 5 balloons burst. She divided the rest equally among her 6 nieces. How many balloons did each niece receive?

Before Balloons

After Balloons

$(m - 5)$ balloons divided among 6 nieces   5 balloons burst

> 6 units represent $(m - 5)$ balloons

From the bar model, number of balloons each niece received:

$\frac{1}{6}(m - 5) = \frac{1}{6}m - \frac{5}{6}$ Use the distributive property.

Each niece received $\underline{\left(\frac{1}{6}m - \frac{5}{6}\right)}$ balloons.

Name: _____ Date: _____

Complete.

4. Felicia drew an isosceles triangle with a base length of 3x inches and side lengths of $\left(\frac{1}{4}x + 3\right)$ inches. Write an algebraic expression for the perimeter of the triangle.

   Perimeter of the triangle:

   _____ + _____ + _____

   = _____

   The perimeter of the triangle is _____ inches.

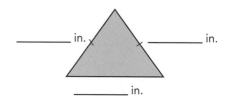

_____ in. _____ in.

_____ in.

Solve. You may use a diagram, model, or table.

5. The admission fees to an amusement theme park are $45 per adult and $25 per child. A tour group of 2x adults and (3x − 8) children visited the park. How much did the tour group pay in total?

6. A one-way train ticket from New York to Los Angeles costs $197 for a reclining seat, and $490 for a twin-sharing room. How much would it cost if x passengers booked reclining seats and $\frac{1}{5}y$ passengers booked twin-sharing rooms?

7. Colin had x dollars to spend in a week. He spent $20 on Monday and on Tuesday. He then spent the rest equally on each day for the rest of the week. How much did Colin spend on Thursday?

Name: _____ Date: _____

Lesson 3.7 Real-World Problems: Algebraic Reasoning

Solve a real-world ratio problem involving algebraic expressions.

Example

Bella has y meters of fabric. She uses 4 meters to make a banner. She then cuts the remaining fabric into 2 pieces in the ratio 1 : 3. What is the length of the shorter piece of fabric?

Method 1
Use a bar model.

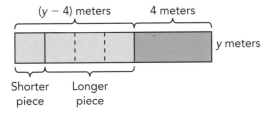

($y - 4$) meters   4 meters

y meters

Shorter   Longer
piece   piece

From the bar model, the length of the shorter piece is:

$$\frac{1}{4}(y - 4) = \frac{1}{4}y - 1 \qquad \text{Use the distributive property.}$$

The shorter piece is $\left(\frac{1}{4}y - 1\right)$ meters.

Method 2
Use algebraic reasoning.

Only the remaining cloth is cut into 2 pieces. So, subtract 4 meters from y meters.

Shorter piece : Longer piece
     1 : 3

So, the shorter piece is $\frac{1}{4}$ the length of the remaining fabric.

Length of remaining fabric:
$y - 4$

Length of the shorter piece:

$$\frac{1}{4}(y - 4) = \frac{1}{4}(y) - \frac{1}{4}(4) \qquad \text{Use the distributive property.}$$

$$= \frac{1}{4}y - 1$$

The shorter piece is $\left(\frac{1}{4}y - 1\right)$ meters.

Complete.

1. On Monday morning, James walked $\left(\frac{1}{8}y + 8\right)$ miles from his house to the park.

   At the park, he jogged 3 times the distance from his house to the park. After his jog, he walked home by the same route. Find the total distance he walked and jogged that morning.

   Total distance jogged:

   $$\underline{\hspace{1.5cm}} \left(\frac{1}{8}y + 8\right) = \underline{\hspace{1cm}}(\underline{\hspace{1cm}}) + \underline{\hspace{1cm}}(\underline{\hspace{1cm}}) \quad \text{Use the distributive property.}$$

   $$= \underline{\hspace{1.5cm}} + \underline{\hspace{1.5cm}} \quad \text{Multiply.}$$

   He walked and jogged a total distance of _____ miles.

Solve each question by algebraic reasoning.

2. If the average daily rainfall for the last 7 days was (3x + 0.5) centimetres, write an algebraic expression for the total rainfall for the whole week.

3. The area of a rectangle is (2x + 15) square centimeters. The ratio of the shaded region to the unshaded region is 3 : 2. Write an algebraic expression for the area of the shaded region in terms of x.

4. A drawer contained 49 pencils and erasers. Will removed p pencils from the drawer. The remaining pencils and erasers were in the ratio 2 : 5. Write an algebraic expression for the number of pencils left in the drawer.

Name: _____   Date: _____

Solve a word problem involving algebraic expressions.

Example

Tim is x years old. His father is $\left(\frac{5x}{2} + 6\right)$ years old. His mother is $\frac{x}{5}$ years younger than his father. Express the sum of their ages in terms of x.

Tim's age   Father's age   Mother's age

Sum of their ages: $x + \left(\frac{5x}{2} + 6\right) + \left(\frac{5x}{2} + 6 - \frac{x}{5}\right)$ Write the addition expression.

$= x + \frac{5}{2}x + 6 + \frac{5}{2}x + 6 - \frac{1}{5}x$ Rewrite the expression.

$= x + \frac{5}{2}x + \frac{5}{2}x - \frac{1}{5}x + 6 + 6$ Group like terms.

$= \frac{10}{10}x + \frac{25}{10}x + \frac{25}{10}x - \frac{2}{10}x + 6 + 6$ LCM of 2 and 5 is 10.

$= \frac{58}{10}x + 12$ Simplify.

The sum of their ages is $\underline{\left(\frac{58}{10}x + 12\right)}$ years.

Complete.

5. Adeline has $2m$ dollars, Bill has $\left(\frac{3m}{2} - 5\right)$ dollars, and Celia has $\frac{m}{6}$ dollars more than Bill. Express the total sum of money Adeline, Bill, and Celia have in terms of m.

Sum of money: $2m + \left(\frac{3m}{2} - 5\right) + ($ _____ $)$ Write the addition expression.

$= 2m + \frac{3}{2}m - 5 +$ _____   Rewrite the expression.

$= 2m + \frac{3}{2}m +$ _____   Group like terms.

$=$ _____   LCM of 2 and 6 is _____ .

$=$ _____   Simplify.

The total sum of money Adeline, Bill, and Celia have is _____ dollars.

Name: _____   Date: _____

Solve each question by algebraic reasoning.

6. Tiffany read $\frac{x}{3}$ books last month. Her brother read $\left(\frac{4}{9}x - 15\right)$ books and her sister read $\frac{x}{9}$ fewer books than Tiffany. Express the total number of books read in terms of x.

7. On a train, there are 2x adults, $\left(\frac{5}{6}q + 10\right)$ teenagers, and 50 fewer toddlers than adults. How many passengers are on the train?

8. The price of a movie ticket is $7 on a weekday. During the weekend, a movie ticket costs 1.2 times the weekday price. During a particular week, m tickets were sold on weekdays and w tickets were sold during the weekend. What is the total amount of money earned from the sale of tickets during that week?

9. One-third of the pears in a basket were rotten. After the rotten pears were thrown away, there were still p pears and q oranges left in the fruit basket. How many total pears and oranges were there in the fruit basket to start with?

Name: _____ Date: _____

4 Algebraic Equations and Inequalities

Lesson 4.1 Understanding Equivalent Equations

Solve each equation.

1. $x + 3 = 5$

2. $2x - 1 = 4$

3. $\frac{1}{2}y = 3$

4. $5y = 3$

State whether each statement is true or false.

5. $x = 0$ gives the solution of the algebraic equation $2x = 3x$. _____

6. $x = 1$ gives the solution of the algebraic equation $2x + 1 = 3$. _____

7. $y = 2$ gives the solution of the algebraic equation $y + 3 = 5$. _____

8. $y = 3$ gives the solution of the algebraic equation $2y + 2 = 4$. _____

Draw a number line to represent each inequality.

9. $x \geq 1.5$

10. $x < 2$

11. $y < \frac{1}{3}$

12. $y \geq 0$

Use _x_ to represent the unknown quantity.
Write an algebraic inequality for each statement.

13. The wooden tray can hold at most 15 pounds.

14. You have to be at least 18 years old to vote in the U.S.

15. The maximum height of all of the ceramic vases on display is 20 inches.

16. There are more than 30 students attending the study session.

State whether each pair of equations are equivalent equations. Give a reason for your answer.

Example

a) $x + 2 + 3x = 6$ and $4x + 2 = 6$

$x + 2 + 3x = 6$
$x + 3x + 2 = 6$ Use the commutative property to group like terms.
$\quad\, 4x + 2 = 6$ Add like terms.

$\underline{x + 2 + 3x = 6}$ can be rewritten as $\underline{4x + 2 = 6}$ using familiar number properties.
So, the equations have the <u>same</u> solution and are <u>equivalent</u>.

b) $3x - 3 = 7$ and $3x = 9$

$\quad\quad\, 3x = 9$
$3x \div 3 = 9 \div 3$ Divide both sides by 3.
$\quad\quad\, x = 3$ Simplify.

Then check to see if 3 is the solution of the equation $3x - 3 = 7$.

If $x = 3, 3x - 3 = 3 \cdot 3 - 3$ Substitute 3 for x.
$\quad\quad\quad\quad = 6\ (\neq 7)$ 3 is not a solution.

Because the equations have <u>different</u> solutions, they are <u>not equivalent</u> equations.
So, $3x - 3 = 7$ and $3x = 9$ are <u>not equivalent</u> equations.

c) $\frac{3}{4}x = 6$ and $x = 8$

If $x = 8, \frac{3}{4}x = \frac{3}{4} \cdot 8$ Substitute 8 for x.
$\quad\quad\quad\quad = 6$ 8 is a solution.

Because the equations have the <u>same</u> solution, ___<u>8</u>___, they are <u>equivalent</u> equations.
So, $\frac{3}{4}x = 6$ and $x = 8$ are <u>equivalent</u> equations.

Complete.

17. $2x - 1 + 3x = 4$ and $5x = 5$

$$2x - 1 + 3x = 4$$

$$5x - 1 = 4 \qquad\qquad \text{Group like terms.}$$

$5x - 1 + \underline{\hspace{1cm}} = 4 + \underline{\hspace{1cm}} \qquad$ Add _____ to both sides.

$$5x = \underline{\hspace{1cm}}$$

Because $2x - 1 + 3x = 5$ _____ be rewritten as $5x = 5$, the equations

are _____.

18. $\frac{3}{5}x = 6$ and $3x = 15$

$$3x = 15$$

$3x \div \underline{\hspace{1cm}} = 15 \div \underline{\hspace{1cm}} \qquad$ Divide both sides by _____.

$$x = \underline{\hspace{1cm}} \qquad\qquad \text{Simplify.}$$

Then check to see if _____ is the solution of the equation $\frac{3}{5}x = 6$.

If $x = \underline{\hspace{1cm}}$, $\frac{3}{5}x = \frac{3}{5} \cdot \underline{\hspace{1cm}}$

$$= \underline{\hspace{1cm}}$$

Because the equations have _____ solutions, they are _____
equations.

So, $\frac{3}{5}x = 6$ and $3x = 15$ are _____ equations.

State whether each pair of equations are equivalent equations. Give a reason for your answer.

19. $4x + 1 - 2x = 7$ and $x = 3$

20. $5x + 2 - 3x = 2$ and $x = 1$

Name: _____   Date: _____

Lesson 4.2   Solving Algebraic Equations

Solve the algebraic equation with variables on the same side of the equation.

Example

$2x - 3 = 5$

$$2x - 3 = 5$$
$$2x - 3 + 3 = 5 + 3 \qquad \text{Add 3 to both sides.}$$
$$2x = 8 \qquad \text{Simplify.}$$
$$2x \div 2 = 8 \div 2 \qquad \text{Divide both sides by 2.}$$
$$x = 4 \qquad \text{Simplify.}$$

$x = \underline{\quad 4 \quad}$ gives the solution of the equation $2x - 3 = 5$.

Check: Substitute the value of $x = 4$ into the original equation.

$$2x - 3 = 2 \cdot 4 - 3$$
$$= 5$$

When $x = \underline{\quad 4 \quad}$, the equation $2x - 3 = 5$ is $\underline{\quad \text{true} \quad}$.

$x = \underline{\quad 4 \quad}$ gives the solution.

Complete.

1. $6 + 8x = 24$

$$6 + 8x = 24$$

$6 + 8x - \underline{\qquad} = 24 - \underline{\qquad}$ Subtract _____ from both sides.

$8x = \underline{\qquad}$ Simplify.

$8x \div \underline{\qquad} = \underline{\qquad} \div \underline{\qquad}$ Divide both sides by _____.

$x = \underline{\qquad}$ Simplify.

$x = \underline{\qquad}$ gives the solution of the equation $6 + 8x = 24$.

Check: Substitute the value of $x = \underline{\qquad}$ into the original equation.

$6 + 8x = 6 + 8 \cdot \underline{\qquad} = \underline{\qquad}$

When $x = \underline{\qquad}$, the equation $6 + 8x = 24$ is _____.

$x = \underline{\qquad}$ gives the solution.

Solve each equation with variables on the same side.

2. $4 - 12x = 20$

3. $-5y - 5 = 10$

Solve the algebraic equation with variables on the same side of the equation.

Example

$\frac{2}{5}x + \frac{1}{2} = 2$

Method 1
Solve by balancing the equation.

$$\frac{2}{5}x + \frac{1}{2} = 2$$

$$\frac{2}{5}x + \frac{1}{2} - \frac{1}{2} = 2 - \frac{1}{2}$$ Subtract $\frac{1}{2}$ from both sides.

$$\frac{2}{5}x = \frac{3}{2}$$ Simplify.

$$\frac{5}{2} \cdot \left(\frac{2}{5}x\right) = \frac{5}{2} \cdot \left(\frac{3}{2}\right)$$ Multiply both sides by $\frac{5}{2}$, which is the reciprocal of the coefficient $\frac{2}{5}$.

$$x = \frac{15}{4}$$ Simplify.

Example

Method 2

Solve by multiplying the equation by the least common denominator (LCD).

$$\frac{2}{5}x + \frac{1}{2} = 2$$

$$10 \cdot \left(\frac{2}{5}x + \frac{1}{2}\right) = 10 \cdot 2 \qquad \text{Multiply both sides by 10, the LCD of } \frac{2}{5} \text{ and } \frac{1}{2}.$$

$$10 \cdot \frac{2}{5}x + 10 \cdot \frac{1}{2} = 10 \cdot 2 \qquad \text{Use the distributive property.}$$

$$4x + 5 = 20 \qquad \text{Simplify.}$$

$$4x + 5 - 5 = 20 - 5 \qquad \text{Subtract 5 from both sides.}$$

$$4x = 15$$

$$4x \div 4 = 15 \div 4 \qquad \text{Divide both sides by 4.}$$

$$x = \frac{15}{4} \qquad \text{Simplify.}$$

$x = \underline{\dfrac{15}{4}}$ gives the solution of the equation $\frac{2}{5}x + \frac{1}{2} = 2$.

Check: Substitute the value of $x = \frac{15}{4}$ into the original equation.

$$\frac{2}{5}x + \frac{1}{2} = \frac{2}{5} \cdot \frac{15}{4} + \frac{1}{2}$$

$$= \frac{3}{2} + \frac{1}{2}$$

$$= 2$$

When $x = \underline{\dfrac{15}{4}}$, the equation $\frac{2}{5}x + \frac{1}{2} = 2$ is __true__. $x = \frac{15}{4}$ gives the solution.

Complete.

4. $\dfrac{1}{3}x + \dfrac{1}{6} = \dfrac{1}{2}$

Method 1

Solve by balancing the equation.

$$\frac{1}{3}x + \frac{1}{6} = \frac{1}{2}$$

$$\frac{1}{3}x + \frac{1}{6} - \underline{\hspace{1.5cm}} = \frac{1}{2} - \underline{\hspace{1.5cm}} \qquad \text{Subtract } \underline{\hspace{1.5cm}} \text{ from both sides.}$$

$$\frac{1}{3}x = \underline{\hspace{1.5cm}} \qquad \text{Simplify.}$$

$$\underline{\hspace{1.5cm}} \cdot \left(\frac{1}{3}x\right) = \underline{\hspace{1.5cm}} \cdot \underline{\hspace{1.5cm}} \qquad \text{Multiply both sides by } \underline{\hspace{1.5cm}}.$$

$$x = \underline{\hspace{1.5cm}} \qquad \text{Simplify.}$$

Method 2
Solve by multiplying the equation by the least common denominator (LCD).

$$\frac{1}{3}x + \frac{1}{6} = \frac{1}{2}$$

$$\underline{\quad\quad} \cdot \left(\frac{1}{3}x + \frac{1}{6}\right) = \underline{\quad\quad} \cdot \left(\frac{1}{2}\right)$$ Multiply both sides by LCD _____ .

$$\underline{\quad\quad} \cdot \frac{1}{3}x + \underline{\quad\quad} \cdot \frac{1}{6} = \underline{\quad\quad} \cdot \left(\frac{1}{2}\right)$$ Use the distributive property.

$$2x + \underline{\quad\quad} = \underline{\quad\quad}$$ Simplify.

$$2x + \underline{\quad\quad} - \underline{\quad\quad} = \underline{\quad\quad} - \underline{\quad\quad}$$ Subtract _____ from both sides.

$$2x = \underline{\quad\quad}$$ Simplify.

$$2x \div \underline{\quad\quad} = \underline{\quad\quad} \div \underline{\quad\quad}$$ Divide both sides by _____ .

$$x = \underline{\quad\quad}$$

$x = \underline{\quad\quad}$ gives the solution of the equation $\frac{1}{3}x + \frac{1}{6} = \frac{1}{2}$.

Check: Substitute the value of $x = \underline{\quad\quad}$ into the original equation.

$$\frac{1}{3}x + \frac{1}{6} = \frac{1}{3} \cdot \underline{\quad\quad} + \frac{1}{6} = \underline{\quad\quad}$$

When $x = \underline{\quad\quad}$, the equation $\frac{1}{3}x + \frac{1}{6} = \frac{1}{2}$ is _____. $x = \underline{\quad\quad}$ gives the solution.

Solve each equation with variables on the same side.

5. $\frac{2}{5}x + \frac{1}{10} = \frac{1}{5}$

6. $\frac{1}{8} - \frac{2}{3}w = \frac{3}{4}$

Solve the algebraic equation with variables on the same side of the equation.

> **Example**
>
> $x - 1.3 + 0.3x = 2.6$
>
> | | |
> |---|---|
> | $x - 1.3 + 0.3x = 2.6$ | |
> | $1.3x - 1.3 = 2.6$ | Subtract the like terms. |
> | $1.3x - 1.3 + 1.3 = 2.6 + 1.3$ | Add 1.3 to both sides. |
> | $1.3x = 3.9$ | Simplify. |
> | $1.3x \div 1.3 = 3.9 \div 1.3$ | Divide both sides by 1.3. |
> | $x = 3$ | Simplify. |

Complete.

7. $0.4x - 3 + 1.2x = 0.6$

$0.4x - 3 + 1.2x = 0.6$	
$\underline{\hspace{2cm}} - 3 = 0.6$	Group like terms.
$\underline{\hspace{2cm}} - 3 + \underline{\hspace{1.5cm}} = 0.6 + \underline{\hspace{1.5cm}}$	Add $\underline{\hspace{1.5cm}}$ to both sides.
$\underline{\hspace{2cm}} = \underline{\hspace{1.5cm}}$	Simplify.
$\underline{\hspace{2cm}} = \underline{\hspace{1.5cm}}$	Divide both sides by $\underline{\hspace{1.5cm}}$.
$x = \underline{\hspace{1.5cm}}$	Simplify.

Solve each equation with variables on the same side.

8. $0.3x - 0.1 + 0.2x = 1.4$

9. $y - 1 - 0.6y = 2.4$

Solve the algebraic equation with variables on both sides of the equation.

Example

$3 - 4x = 2x + 11$

Method 1
Isolate the variable on the left side of the equation.

$3 - 4x = 2x + 11$	
$3 - 4x - 2x = 2x + 11 - 2x$	Subtract 2x from both sides.
$3 - 6x = 11$	Simplify.
$3 - 6x - 3 = 11 - 3$	Subtract 3 to both sides.
$-6x = 8$	Simplify.
$\dfrac{-6x}{-6} = \dfrac{8}{-6}$	Divide both sides by −6.
$x = -\dfrac{4}{3}$	Simplify.

Method 2
Isolate the variable on the right side of the equation.

$3 - 4x = 2x + 11$	
$3 - 4x + 4x = 2x + 11 + 4x$	Add 4x to both sides.
$3 = 11 + 6x$	Simplify.
$3 - 11 = 11 + 6x - 11$	Subtract 11 from both sides.
$-8 = 6x$	Simplify.
$\dfrac{-8}{6} = \dfrac{6x}{6}$	Divide both sides by 6.
$-\dfrac{4}{3} = x$	Simplify.

> Remember to check your solution by substituting the solution $x = -\dfrac{4}{3}$ into the original equation.

Complete.

10. $10 - 4x = 2x + 16$

$10 - 4x - \underline{\hspace{1cm}} = 2x + 16 - \underline{\hspace{1cm}}$	Subtract 2x from both sides.
$10 - \underline{\hspace{1cm}} = 16$	Simplify.
$10 - \underline{\hspace{1cm}} - \underline{\hspace{1cm}} = 16 - \underline{\hspace{1cm}}$	Subtract 10 from both sides.
$\underline{\hspace{1cm}} = 6$	Simplify.
$\underline{\hspace{1cm}} = \underline{\hspace{1cm}}$	Divide both sides by _____.
$x = \underline{\hspace{1cm}}$	Simplify.

Name: _____   Date: _____

Solve each equation with variables on both sides.

11. $3x - 5 = x + 1$

12. $10 + 2y = 4 - 3y$

Solve the equation with variables on both sides.

─── *Example* ───

$1.7x - 1.1 = 0.9x + 0.5$

$1.7x - 1.1 = 0.9x + 0.5$	Isolate the variable on the left side.
$1.7x - 1.1 - 0.9x = 0.9x + 0.5 - 0.9x$	Subtract 0.9x from both sides.
$0.8x - 1.1 = 0.5$	Simplify.
$0.8x - 1.1 + 1.1 = 0.5 + 1.1$	Add 1.1 to both sides.
$0.8x = 1.6$	Simplify.
$\dfrac{0.8x}{0.8} = \dfrac{1.6}{0.8}$	Divide both sides by 0.8.
$x = 2$	Simplify.

13. $3.1y + 1.2 = 2.3y + 2.8$

14. $1.2 - 3.2p = 5.2p + 4$

15. $4.2m - 0.6 = -1 - 1.8m$

16. $6.3 + 1.5w = 5w - 0.7$

Solve the algebraic equation with variables on both sides of the equation.

Example

$$\frac{5}{6}m - \frac{1}{3} = \frac{3}{4}m + \frac{1}{2}$$

Method 1

Solve by balancing the equation.

$$\frac{5}{6}m - \frac{1}{3} = \frac{3}{4}m + \frac{1}{2}$$

$$\frac{5}{6}m - \frac{1}{3} - \frac{3}{4}m = \frac{3}{4}m + \frac{1}{2} - \frac{3}{4}m \qquad \text{Subtract } \frac{3}{4}m \text{ from both sides.}$$

$$\frac{10}{12}m - \frac{1}{3} - \frac{9}{12}m = \frac{1}{2} \qquad \text{The LCD of } \frac{5}{6} \text{ and } \frac{3}{4} \text{ is 12. } \frac{5}{6}m = \frac{10}{12}m; \frac{3}{4}m = \frac{9}{12}m.$$

$$\frac{1}{12}m - \frac{1}{3} = \frac{1}{2} \qquad \text{Subtract the like terms.}$$

$$\frac{1}{12}m - \frac{1}{3} + \frac{1}{3} = \frac{1}{2} + \frac{1}{3} \qquad \text{Add } \frac{1}{3} \text{ to both sides.}$$

$$\frac{1}{12}m = \frac{5}{6} \qquad \text{Simplify.}$$

$$12 \cdot \frac{1}{12}m = 12 \cdot \frac{5}{6} \qquad \text{Multiply both sides by the reciprocal of } \frac{1}{12}, 12.$$

$$m = 10$$

Method 2

Solve by multiplying both sides of the equation by the LCD.

$$\frac{5}{6}m - \frac{1}{3} = \frac{3}{4}m + \frac{1}{2}$$

$$12 \cdot \left(\frac{5}{6}m - \frac{1}{3}\right) = 12 \cdot \left(\frac{3}{4}m + \frac{1}{2}\right) \qquad \text{Multiply both sides by 12, the LCD of } \frac{5}{6}, \frac{1}{3}, \frac{3}{4}, \text{ and } \frac{1}{2}.$$

$$12 \cdot \frac{5}{6}m - 12 \cdot \frac{1}{3} = 12 \cdot \frac{3}{4}m + 12 \cdot \frac{1}{2} \qquad \text{Use the distributive property.}$$

$$10m - 4 = 9m + 6 \qquad \text{Simplify.}$$

$$10m - 4 - 9m = 9m + 6 - 9m \qquad \text{Subtract } 9m \text{ from both sides.}$$

$$m - 4 = 6 \qquad \text{Simplify.}$$

$$m - 4 + 4 = 6 + 4 \qquad \text{Add 4 to both sides.}$$

$$m = 10 \qquad \text{Simplify.}$$

Remember to check your solution by substituting the solution $m = 10$ into the original equation.

Name: _____   Date: _____

Complete.

17. $\frac{2}{7}y + 1 = \frac{3}{14}y - \frac{1}{2}$

$\frac{2}{7}y + 1 - \underline{\hspace{1cm}} = \frac{3}{14}y - \frac{1}{2} - \underline{\hspace{1cm}}$ Subtract $\frac{3}{14}y$ from both sides.

$\underline{\hspace{1cm}} + 1 - \underline{\hspace{1cm}} = -\frac{1}{2}$ The LCD of $\frac{2}{7}$ and $\frac{3}{14}$ is 14. $\frac{2}{7}y = \underline{\hspace{1cm}}$.

$\underline{\hspace{1cm}} + 1 = -\frac{1}{2}$ Group like terms.

$\underline{\hspace{1cm}} + 1 - \underline{\hspace{1cm}} = -\frac{1}{2} - \underline{\hspace{1cm}}$ Subtract 1 from both sides.

$\underline{\hspace{1cm}}y = \underline{\hspace{1cm}}$ Simplify.

$\underline{\hspace{1cm}} \cdot (\underline{\hspace{1cm}}y) = \underline{\hspace{1cm}} \cdot (\underline{\hspace{1cm}})$ Multiply both sides by _____.

$y = \underline{\hspace{1cm}}$ Simplify.

18. $\frac{1}{10}x - \frac{2}{5} = \frac{3}{4}x + \frac{1}{4}$

$\underline{\hspace{1cm}} \cdot \left(\frac{1}{10}x - \frac{2}{5}\right) = \underline{\hspace{1cm}} \cdot \left(\frac{3}{4}x + \frac{1}{4}\right)$ Multiply both sides by the LCD, _____.

$\underline{\hspace{1cm}} \cdot \frac{1}{10}x - \underline{\hspace{1cm}} \cdot \frac{2}{5} = \underline{\hspace{1cm}} \cdot \frac{3}{4}x + \underline{\hspace{1cm}} \cdot \frac{1}{4}$ Use the distributive property.

$2x - \underline{\hspace{1cm}} = \underline{\hspace{1cm}} + 5$ Simplify.

$2x - \underline{\hspace{1cm}} - \underline{\hspace{1cm}} = \underline{\hspace{1cm}} + 5 - \underline{\hspace{1cm}}$ Subtract 2x from both sides.

$-8 = \underline{\hspace{1cm}} + 5$ Simplify.

$-8 - 5 = \underline{\hspace{1cm}} + 5 - \underline{\hspace{1cm}}$ Subtract 5 from both sides.

$-13 = \underline{\hspace{1cm}} x$ Simplify.

$\underline{\hspace{1cm}} = \underline{\hspace{1cm}}$ Divide both sides by _____.

$\underline{\hspace{1cm}} = x$ Simplify.

Solve each equation with variables on both sides.

19. $\frac{3}{4}p - \frac{1}{2} = \frac{3}{8}p + 1$ **20.** $\frac{2}{5} - \frac{1}{6}y = \frac{3}{10} + \frac{4}{6}y$

Name: _____   Date: _____

Solve the algebraic equation in factored form.

Example

$\frac{1}{5}(x + 2) = 2$

Method 1
Use the distributive property and inverse operations.

$\frac{1}{5}(x + 2) = 2$

$\frac{1}{5} \cdot x + \frac{1}{5} \cdot 2 = 2$ Use the distributive property.

$\frac{1}{5}x + \frac{2}{5} = 2$ Simplify.

$\frac{1}{5}x + \frac{2}{5} - \frac{2}{5} = \frac{10}{5} - \frac{2}{5}$ Subtract $\frac{2}{5}$ from both sides. Rewrite 2 as $\frac{10}{5}$.

$\frac{1}{5}x = \frac{8}{5}$ Simplify.

$5 \cdot \frac{1}{5}x = 5 \cdot \frac{8}{5}$ Multiply both sides by 5.

$x = 8$ Simplify. Express in simplest form.

Method 2
Use inverse operations.

$\frac{1}{5}(x + 2) = 2$ Multiply both sides by 5.

$5 \cdot \frac{1}{5}(x + 2) = 5 \cdot 2$ Simplify.
        Subtract 2 from both sides.

$x + 2 = 10$ Simplify.

$x + 2 - 2 = 10 - 2$

$x = 8$

Complete.

21. $\frac{1}{3}(2y + 6) = 3$

$\frac{1}{3}(2y + 6) = 3$

_____ $\cdot \frac{1}{3}(2y + 6) =$ _____ $\cdot 3$ Multiply both sides by _____.

$2y +$ _____ $= 9$ Simplify.

$2y +$ _____ $- 6 = 9 -$ _____   Subtract 6 from both sides.

_____ $y =$ _____   Simplify.

_____ $=$ _____   Divide both sides by _____.

$y =$ _____   Simplify.

Solve each equation involving parentheses.

22. $\frac{1}{2}(3x - 4) = 7$

23. $5(m + 4) = 15$

Solve the algebraic equation in factored form.

Example

$2.4 + 1.2(n + 2) = 6$

$2.4 + 1.2 \cdot n + 1.2 \cdot 2 = 6$	Use the distributive property.
$1.2n + 4.8 = 6$	Simplify.
$1.2n + 4.8 - 4.8 = 6 - 4.8$	Subtract 4.8 from both sides.
$1.2n = 1.2$	Simplify.
$\dfrac{1.2n}{1.2} = \dfrac{1.2}{1.2}$	Divide both sides by 1.2.
$n = 1$	Simplify.

Complete.

24. $2x + 4(6 - x) = 30$

$$2x + 4(6 - x) = 30$$

$2x + 4 \cdot \underline{\hspace{1cm}} - 4 \cdot \underline{\hspace{1cm}} = 30$	Use the distributive property.
$2x + \underline{\hspace{1cm}} - \underline{\hspace{1cm}} = 30$	Simplify.
$\underline{\hspace{1cm}} + \underline{\hspace{1cm}} = 30$	Subtract the like terms.
$\underline{\hspace{1cm}} + \underline{\hspace{1cm}} - \underline{\hspace{1cm}} = 30 - \underline{\hspace{1cm}}$	Subtract _____ from both sides.
$\underline{\hspace{1cm}} x = \underline{\hspace{1cm}}$	Simplify.
$\underline{\hspace{1cm}} = \underline{\hspace{1cm}}$	Divide both sides by _____.
$x = \underline{\hspace{1cm}}$	Simplify.

Solve each equation involving parentheses.

25. $2y + 3(y - 2) = -1$

26. $3(2p - 1) - 5p = 4$

Name: _____   Date: _____

Lesson 4.3 Real-World Problems: Algebraic Equations

Solve the word problem using bar models and algebraic reasoning .

> *Example*
>
> Linda is three times as old as Isabelle. The difference between their ages is 18.
> Find the age of Linda and Isabelle.
>
> **Method 1**
> Use bar models.
>
>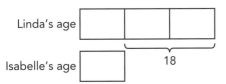
>
> Linda's age
>
> Isabelle's age   18
>
> From the bar models,
> 2 units → ___18___
>
> 1 unit → __2__ ÷ __2__ = __9__
>
> 3 units → __9__ · __3__ = __27__
>
> Linda is _27 years old_ and
>
> Isabelle is _9 years old_.
>
> **Method 2**
> Use algebraic reasoning.
>
> Let Isabelle's age be x.
> Then Linda's age is 3x.
>
> $3x - x = 18$
> $2x = 18$
> $\dfrac{2x}{2} = \dfrac{18}{2}$
> $x = 9$
>
> Find Linda's age: $3x = 3 \cdot 9$
> $= 27$
>
> Linda is _27 years old_ and
>
> Isabelle is _9 years old_.

Complete.

1. Mark recorded two temperature measurements for his experiment. One of the
    measurements is $\frac{2}{3}$ of the other measurement. If the sum of the measurements
    is −30°C, what two measurements were recorded?

    Let one measurement be y. Then the other measurement is $\frac{2}{3}\,y$.

    _____ $+ \frac{2}{3}\,y = -30$ Write an equation.

    _____$y = -30$ Simplify.

    _____ · _____ $y =$ _____ $\cdot (-30)$ Multiply both sides by the reciprocal of $\frac{5}{3}$, _____.

    $y =$ _____   Simplify.

    The other temperature:

    $\frac{2}{3}\,y = \frac{2}{3} \cdot$ _____ $=$ _____   Evaluate $\frac{2}{3}y$ when $y =$ _____.

    The two measurements recorded were _____°C and _____°C.

Name: _____ Date: _____

Solve.

2. Melissa has twice as many pencils as Elle. The difference in pencils is 15. How many pencils does each of the girls have?

3. Logan sold three times as many oranges as apples. The total number of oranges and apples sold is 88. Find the number of apples and oranges sold.

Solve.

Example

Three different courses are held in a school. There are 358 participants for Course A while there are x participants for each of Courses B and C. The fees for Course A is $220 per participant while the course fee for each participant for Courses B and C is $150.

a) Write an expression for the total amount of course fees.

Organize the information into a table.

Course	Course Fee ($)	Number of Participants	Total Amount ($)
A	220	358	$220 \cdot 358 = 78{,}760$
B	150	x	$150 \cdot x = 150x$
C	150	x	$150 \cdot x = 150x$

From the table, the total course fees is $\underline{(78{,}760 + 300x)}$ dollars.

b) If the total amount of course fees is $174,760, how many participants are there for Course B?

$$78{,}760 + 300x = 174{,}760 \qquad \text{Write an equation.}$$
$$78{,}760 + 300x - 78{,}760 = 174{,}760 - 78{,}760 \qquad \text{Subtract 78,760 from both sides.}$$
$$300x = 96{,}000 \qquad \text{Simplify.}$$
$$\frac{300x}{300} = \frac{96{,}000}{300} \qquad \text{Divide both sides by 300.}$$
$$x = 320 \qquad \text{Simplify.}$$

There are __320__ participants in Course B.

Name: _____   Date: _____

Complete.

4. The tickets sold for a train ride are divided into two categories — "premiere seats" and "economical seats". The premiere seat costs $120 each and the economical seat costs $75 each. There are 375 premiere seats and x economical seats on a train.

   a) If the train is sold out, write an expression for the total amount of ticket sales for the train ride.

Seats	Price	Number of Seats	Total Sale
Premiere			
Economical			

   From the table, the total amount of ticket sales is _____ dollars.

   b) If the total amount of ticket sales when the train is sold out is $86,250, how many tickets for economical seats were sold?

   _____ + _____ = 86,250   Write an equation.

   _____ + _____ − _____ = 86,250 − _____   Subtract _____ from both sides.

   _____ x = _____   Simplify.

   _____ = _____   Divide both sides by _____.

   x = _____   Simplify.

   There were _____ tickets for economical seats sold.

Solve.

5. For a championship baseball game, tickets are priced at $205 for front row seats and $125 for all other seats. There are x front row seats and 2,200 other seats in the stadium.

   a) Write an expression for the total amount of ticket sales if all of the seats are sold out for the game.

   b) If the total amount of money earned from the sale of a sold-out stadium is $500,500, how many front row seats are in the stadium?

Name: _____ Date: _____

Solve.

6. The tickets for a live concert are sold in two different categories. The cost of a ticket in the standing area in front of the stage costs $210 while the cost of a ticket for a seat costs $130. The area in front of the stage can hold 350 people and there are y seats in the arena available.

   a) Write an expression for the total amount of ticket sales if the concert is sold out.

   b) If the total amount of money earned from the sale of a sold-out concert is $164,500, how many seats are in the arena?

Solve the real-world problem algebraically.

> **Example**
>
> Jarrod saved $20 more than Jacob. If they saved $78 altogether, how much did Jacob save?
>
> Let m be the amount of money Jarrod saved.
> Then the amount of money Jacob saved is $m - 20$.
>
> Because they saved $78 altogether,
>
> | | |
> |---|---|
> | $m + (m - 20) = 78$ | Write an equation. |
> | $2m - 20 = 78$ | Simplify. |
> | $2m - 20 + 20 = 78 + 20$ | Add 20 to both sides. |
> | $2m = 98$ | Simplify. |
> | $\dfrac{2m}{2} = \dfrac{98}{2}$ | Divide both sides by 2. |
> | $m = 49$ | Simplify. |
>
> Amount of money Jacob saved: $m - 20 = 49 - 20$
> $\qquad\qquad\qquad\qquad\qquad = 29$ Evaluate $m - 20$ when $m = 49$.
>
> Jacob saved __$29__ .

Name: _____   Date: _____

Complete.

7. Jamie scored 5 points more than Jasmine on a class test. If they scored a total of 153 points, what was Jamie's score?

   Let Jasmine's score be y.
   Then Jamie's score is $y +$ _____.

   Because they scored a total of 153 points,

$y + (y +$ _____$) = 153$	Write an equation.
_____ $+$ _____ $= 153$	Simplify.
_____ $+$ _____ $-$ _____ $= 153 -$ _____	Subtract _____ from both sides.
_____ $y =$ _____	Simplify.
_____ $=$ _____	Divide both sides by _____.
$y =$ _____	Simplify.

   Jamie's score: $y +$ _____ $=$ _____ $+$ _____

   $=$ _____

   Jamie scored _____ points on the test.

Solve.

8. Tommy is 22 years older than his son, Patrick. If their ages add up to 50, how old is Tommy?

9. After school, Kate takes a train and then a bus to get to her home. The train ride is 40 minutes longer than the bus ride. The total traveling duration is $1\frac{1}{3}$ hours. How long is the bus ride?

Lesson 4.4 Solving Algebraic Inequalities

Solve the inequality using addition and subtraction. Then graph the solution set on a number line.

Example

$0.4x - 6 + 0.6x > 10$

$$0.4x - 6 + 0.6x > 10$$
$$x - 6 > 10 \qquad \text{Add the like terms.}$$
$$x - 6 + 6 > 10 + 6 \qquad \text{Add 6 to both sides.}$$
$$x > 16 \qquad \text{Simplify.}$$

The solution set is $x > 16$ and it can be represented on a number line as follows:

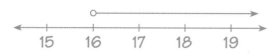

15   16   17   18   19

Check your answer by substituting a number greater than 16 into the original inequality.

Complete. Then graph the solution set on a number line.

1. $1.9x + 2 + 0.1x \le 5$

$$1.9x + 2 + 0.1x \le 5$$
$$\underline{\hspace{1cm}} + 2 \le 5 \qquad \text{Add the like terms.}$$
$$\underline{\hspace{1cm}} + 2 - \underline{\hspace{1cm}} \le 5 - \underline{\hspace{1cm}} \qquad \text{Subtract } \underline{\hspace{1cm}} \text{ from both sides.}$$
$$\underline{\hspace{1cm}} \le \underline{\hspace{1cm}} \qquad \text{Simplify.}$$
$$\underline{\hspace{1cm}} \le \underline{\hspace{1cm}} \qquad \text{Divide both sides by } \underline{\hspace{1cm}}.$$
$$x \le \underline{\hspace{1cm}} \qquad \text{Simplify.}$$

Solve each inequality using addition and subtraction. Then graph the solution set on a number line.

2. $0.3m + 1 + 0.7m \ge 4$

3. $1.4y - 2 + 1.6y < 1$

Name: _____   Date: _____

Solve the inequality using addition and subtraction. Then graph the solution set on a number line.

> **Example**
>
> $\frac{4}{3}y - 2 - \frac{1}{3}y \le 5$
>
> $\frac{4}{3}y - 2 - \frac{1}{3}y \le 5$
>
> $\quad\quad y - 2 \le 5$ Subtract the like terms.
>
> $\quad y - 2 + 2 \le 5 + 2$ Add 2 to both sides.
>
> $\quad\quad\quad y \le 7$ Simplify.
>
> The solution set is $y \le 7$ and it can be represented on a number line as follows:
>
>
>
> ```
>    +----+----+----+----•----+---->
>    4    5    6    7    8
> ```

Complete. Then graph the solution set on a number line.

4. $-\frac{2}{7}y - 4 + \frac{9}{7}y \le 14$

$\quad\quad -\frac{2}{7}y - 4 + \frac{9}{7}y \le 14$

$\quad\quad \underline{\hspace{2cm}} - 4 \le 14$ Subtract the like terms.

$\quad \underline{\hspace{2cm}} -4 + \underline{\hspace{2cm}} \le 14 + \underline{\hspace{2cm}}$ Add $\underline{\hspace{2cm}}$ to both sides.

$\quad\quad \underline{\hspace{2cm}} \le \underline{\hspace{2cm}}$ Simplify.

Solve each inequality using addition and subtraction. Then graph the solution set on a number line.

5. $\frac{3}{4}x + 5 + \frac{1}{4}x < 7$

6. $-\frac{5}{4}w - 10 + \frac{3}{4}w > -2$

Name: _____   Date: _____

Solve the inequality using addition and subtraction. Then graph the solution set on a number line.

Example

$1.2x - 3.8 \leq 7.2 + 0.2x$

$$1.2x - 3.8 \leq 7.2 + 0.2x$$
$$1.2x - 3.8 - 0.2x \leq 7.2 + 0.2x - 0.2x \qquad \text{Subtract } 0.2x \text{ from both sides.}$$
$$x - 3.8 \leq 7.2 \qquad \text{Simplify.}$$
$$x - 3.8 + 3.8 \leq 7.2 + 3.8 \qquad \text{Add 3.8 to both sides.}$$
$$x \leq 11 \qquad \text{Simplify.}$$

The solution set can be represented on a number line as shown:

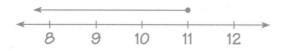

Complete. Then graph the solution set on a number line.

7. $8 + \dfrac{3}{4}m > 11 - \dfrac{1}{4}m$

$$8 + \frac{3}{4}m > 11 - \frac{1}{4}m$$

$$8 + \frac{3}{4}m + \text{_____} > 11 - \frac{1}{4}m + \text{_____} \qquad \text{Add _____ to both sides.}$$

$$8 + \text{_____} > 11 \qquad \text{Simplify.}$$

$$8 + \text{_____} - \text{_____} > 11 - \text{_____} \qquad \text{Subtract _____ from both sides.}$$

$$\text{_____} > \text{_____} \qquad \text{Simplify.}$$

Solve each inequality using addition and subtraction. Then graph the solution set on a number line.

8. $2.8y - 1 > 2 + 1.8y$

9. $\dfrac{9}{8}n + 2 \geq \dfrac{1}{8}n + 8$

Name: _____   Date: _____

Solve the inequality using multiplication. Then graph the solution set on a number line.

Example

$-\dfrac{1}{7}x < 3$

$$-\dfrac{1}{7}x < 3$$

$-\dfrac{1}{7}x \cdot -7 > 3 \cdot -7$ Multiply both sides by -7 and reverse the inequality symbol.

$x > -21$ Simplify.

The solution set can be represented on a number line as shown:

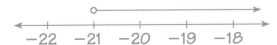

Complete. Then graph the solution set on a number line.

10. $1.5 > -0.3y$

$1.5 > -0.3y$

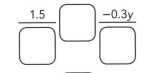

Divide both sides by _____ and reverse the inequality symbol.

_____ ◯ y Simplify.

Solve each inequality using multiplication and division. Then graph the solution set on a number line.

11. $2 < -\dfrac{1}{6}x$

12. $-0.3x \ge 6$

Solve and graph the solution sets of multi-step algebraic inequalities.

Example

$\frac{2}{3}w + 2 > 3\frac{1}{3}$

$\frac{2}{3}w + 2 > 3\frac{1}{3}$

$\frac{2}{3}w + 2 - 2 > 3\frac{1}{3} - 2$ Subtract 2 from both sides.

$\frac{2}{3}w > 1\frac{1}{3}$ Simplify.

$\left(\frac{2}{3}w\right) \cdot \left(\frac{3}{2}\right) > \left(\frac{4}{3}\right) \cdot \left(\frac{3}{2}\right)$ Multiply both sides by $\frac{3}{2}$, which is the reciprocal of $\frac{2}{3}$.

$w > 2$ Simplify.

The solution set can be represented on a number line as shown:

Complete and graph the solution set on a number line.

13. $-2 - 2y < 7 + y$

$-2 - 2y < 7 + y$

$-2 - 2y - y < 7 + y - y$ Subtract _____ from both sides.

$-2 - \text{_____} < 7$ Simplify.

$-2 - \text{_____} + \text{_____} < 7 + \text{_____}$ Add _____ to both sides.

$\text{_____} < \text{_____}$ Simplify.

$\text{_____} > \text{_____}$ Divide both sides by _____ and reverse the inequality symbol.

$y > \text{_____}$ Simplify.

Solve each inequality and graph the solution set on a number line.

14. $-x - 3 > 6 + 2x$

15. $\frac{3}{5}n + 8 > 2\frac{1}{5}n$

Solve and graph the solution sets of multi-step algebraic inequalities.

Example

$3(x + 1) \leq 6$

Method 1
Use the distributive property and inverse operations.

$$3(x + 1) \leq 6$$
$$3 \cdot x + 3 \cdot 1 \leq 6$$
$$3x + 3 \leq 6$$
$$3x + 3 - 3 \leq 6 - 3$$
$$3x \leq 3$$
$$\frac{3x}{3} \leq \frac{3}{3}$$
$$x \leq 1$$

Method 2
Use inverse operations.

$$3(x + 1) \leq 6$$
$$3(x + 1) \div 3 \leq 6 \div 3$$
$$x + 1 \leq 2$$
$$x + 1 - 1 \leq 2 - 1$$
$$x \leq 1$$

The solution set can be represented on a number line as shown:

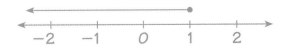

Complete and graph the solution set on a number line.

16. $2(2y + 5) > 6$

$$2(2y + 5) > 6$$

$2(2y + 5) \div$ _____ $> 6 \div$ _____   Divide both sides by 2.

_____ $+ 5 >$ _____   Simplify.

_____ $+ 5 -$ _____ $>$ _____ $- 5$ Subtract 5 from both sides.

_____ $>$ _____   Simplify.

_____ $>$ _____   Divide both sides by _____.

$y >$ _____   Simplify.

Solve each inequality and graph the solution set on a number line.

17. $3(2 + x) < -15$

18. $\frac{1}{3}(2 - x) \leq 1\frac{1}{3}$

Lesson 4.5 Real-World Problems: Algebraic Inequalities

Solve a real-world problem involving algebraic inequalities.

Example

The average age of five people is at least 60 years old. The ages of four of the people are 50, 55, 63, and 60 years old. What is the minimum age of the fifth person?

Let x be the age of the fifth person.   Define the variable.

$$\text{Average} \geq 60$$

$$\frac{50 + 55 + 63 + 60 + x}{5} \geq 60$$ Write an inequality.

$$\frac{228 + x}{5} \geq 60$$ Simplify.

$$5 \cdot \left(\frac{228 + x}{5}\right) \geq 5 \cdot 60$$ Multiply both sides by 5.

$$228 + x \geq 300$$ Simplify.

$$228 + x - 228 \geq 300 - 228$$ Subtract 228 from both sides.

$$x \geq 72$$ Simplify.

The fifth person is at least _72 years old_ .

Complete.

1. The average of 30, 35, 35, 40, and a fifth number is at most 40. What is the maximum value of the fifth number?

   Let x be the fifth number.

   $$\text{Average} \leq 40$$ Define the variable.

   $$\frac{30 + \underline{\quad} + \underline{\quad} + \underline{\quad} + \underline{\quad}}{5} \leq 40$$ Write an inequality.

   $$\underline{\quad\quad} \leq 40$$ Simplify.

   $$5 \cdot (\underline{\quad\quad}) \leq 5 \cdot 40$$ Multiply both sides by 5.

   $$140 + \underline{\quad} \leq \underline{\quad}$$ Simplify.

   $$140 + \underline{\quad} - \underline{\quad} \leq \underline{\quad} - 140$$ Subtract 140 from both sides.

   $$x \leq \underline{\quad}$$ Simplify.

   The value of the fifth number is at most _____.

Solve.

2. Jeremy bought four books. The costs of three books were $10, $13, and $15. The average cost of the four books is at least $14. What is the minimum cost of the fourth book?

3. The average score of six students on a mathematics test is at least 70. Five of the students scored 72, 65, 68, 70, and 78. What is the lowest score of the sixth student?

Solve a real-world problem involving algebraic inequalities.

> **Example**
>
> Kathie buys a bottle of fruit juice for $2.50 and a few loaves of bread for $1.20 each. If she has only $10, at most how many loaves of breads can she buy?
>
> Let y be the number of loaves of breads Kathie can buy.
>
> | | |
> |---|---|
> | $2.5 + 1.2x \leq 10$ | Write an inequality. |
> | $2.5 + 1.2y - 2.5 \leq 10 - 2.5$ | Subtract 2.5 from both sides. |
> | $1.2y \leq 7.5$ | Simplify. |
> | $\dfrac{1.2y}{1.2} \leq \dfrac{7.5}{1.2}$ | Divide both sides by 1.2. |
> | $y \leq 6.25$ | Simplify. |
>
> Kathie can buy at most ____6____ loaves of bread.
>
>
>
> In this case, the greatest number of loaves of bread cannot be a decimal. It must be a whole number.

Complete.

4. Kevin's assignment is to complete a mathematics quiz with 25 multiple-choice questions. For every correct answer, he gets 2 points. One point is deducted for every wrong answer. How many answers must Kevin get correct in order to score more than 30 points?

Let x be the number of correct answers.
Then the number of wrong answers is $25 - x$.

So, the points awarded for correct answers is $2x$ and the scores deducted for wrong answers is $-1(25 - x)$.

$$2x + \text{_____} > 30 \qquad \text{Write an inequality.}$$

$$2x - \text{_____} + \text{_____} > 30$$

$$\text{_____} - \text{_____} > 30 \qquad \text{Simplify.}$$

$$3x - \text{_____} + \text{_____} > 30 + \text{_____} \qquad \text{Add _____ to both sides.}$$

$$\text{_____} > \text{_____} \qquad \text{Simplify.}$$

$$\text{_____} > \text{_____} \qquad \text{Divide both sides by _____.}$$

$$x > \text{_____} \qquad \text{Simplify.}$$

Kevin must get _____ correct answers in order to score more than 30 points.

Solve.

5. Natalia has $20 to spend at a stationery shop. She plans to buy a notebook for $3.50 and some pens for $1.50 each. At most, how many pens can she buy?

6. There are 40 multiple-choice questions on a quiz. A student gets 3 points for every correct answer. One point is deducted for a wrong answer. If a student needs to score at least 100 points to pass the quiz, how many answers must he answer correctly?

Solve a real-world problem involving algebraic inequalities.

Example

Selena would like to sign up for a mobile phone plan and is given two different payment options.

Plan A	Plan B
$0.20 per minute $45 per month	$0.15 per minute $55 per month

After how many minutes of talk-time will Plan B be less expensive than Plan A?

Let x be the number of minutes of talk-time.

$0.2x + 45 > 0.15x + 55$	Write an inequality.
$0.2x + 45 - 0.15x > 0.15x + 55 - 0.15x$	Subtract 0.15x from both sides.
$0.05x + 45 > 55$	Simplify.
$0.05x + 45 - 45 > 55 - 45$	Subtract 45 from both sides.
$0.05x > 10$	Simplify.
$\dfrac{0.05x}{0.05} > \dfrac{10}{0.05}$	Divide both sides by 0.05.
$x > 200$	Simplify.

Plan B will be less expensive than Plan A if the talk-time exceeds __200__ minutes.

Complete.

7. The membership fees for two different movie clubs are provided below.

Best Movie Club	Ultimate Movie Club
$50 administration fee $80 per month	$30 administration fee $100 per month

After how many months will Best Movie Club be less expensive than Ultimate Movie Club?

Let y be the number of months.

$50 + $ _____ $< 30 + $ _____	Write an inequality.
$50 + $ _____ $- $ _____ $< 30 + $ _____ $- $ _____	Subtract _____ from both sides.
$50 - $ _____ < 30	Simplify.
$50 - $ _____ $- $ _____ $< 30 - $ _____	Subtract _____ from both sides.
_____ $< $ _____	Simplify.
_____ $> $ _____	Divide both sides by _____ and reverse the symbol.
$y > $ _____	Simplify.

Best Movie Club will be less expensive than Ultimate Movie Club after _____ month(s).

Solve.

8. Felicia wants to bring some people on a day tour in New York City. She organized the packages from two travel agencies in the table shown.

Travel Agency A	Travel Agency B
$30 per person $65 agency fee	$50 per person $25 agency fee

What is the maximum number of people who can sign up for the trip so that Travel Agency B will be less expensive than Travel Agency A?

9. Emily would like to rent a studio for a dance audition. She was given the following packages to choose from.

Studio A	Studio B
$2,500 for six hours $10 per hour exceeded	$3,000 for six hours $5 per hour exceeded

How many hours would Emily have exceeded at Studio A to incur more cost than at Studio B?

Name: _____   Date: _____

 Direct and Inverse Proportion

Lesson 5.1   Understanding Direct Proportion

Tell whether each ratio is in simplest form. Then write two ratios that are equivalent to the given ratio.

1. 2 : 3

2. 6 : 9

3. 9 : 16

4. 10 : 25

5. 24 : 40

6. 36 : 16

7. 12 : 32

8. 30 : 18

Tell whether _y_ is directly proportional to _x_. If so, find the constant of proportionality.

┌─ _Example_ ───┐

x	1	2	3
y	2	4	6

For each pair of values x and y:

$\dfrac{2}{1} = 2$ $\dfrac{4}{2} = 2$ $\dfrac{6}{3} = 2$

Is y proportional to x? ___Yes___

If yes, what is the constant of proportionality? ___2___

└───┘

Tell whether *y* is directly proportional to *x*. If so, find the constant of proportionality.

9.

x	1	2	3
y	5	10	15

Is y proportional to x? _____

If yes, what is the constant of proportionality? _____

10.

x	1	2	3
y	2	4	8

Is y proportional to x? _____

If yes, what is the constant of proportionality? _____

11.

x	1	2	3
y	8	16	24

Is y proportional to x? _____

If yes, what is the constant of proportionality? _____

Name: _____   Date: _____

Tell whether _y_ is directly proportional to _x_. If so, find the constant of proportionality and write the direct proportion equation.

Example

a) The table shows the amount of money, _y_ dollars, Daniel earns in _x_ hours.

Time (_x_ hours)	1	2	3
Amount Earned (_y_ dollars)	9	18	27

For each pair of values, _x_ and _y_:

$$\frac{\$9}{1\,h} = \frac{\$18}{2\,h} = \frac{\$27}{3\,h} = \underline{\quad 9 \quad}$$

Is the amount Daniel earned directly proportional to the number of hours he

worked? ___Yes___

If so, what is the constant of proportionality? ___9___

What does this value represent?

It represents the amount of money he earns per hour.

Write the direct proportion equation. _y = 9x_

b) Daniel's pay was adjusted after he worked for a year. The table shows the amount of money, _y_, he earns now in _x_ hours.

Number of Hours (_x_)	2	3	4
Amount Earned (_y_ dollars)	20	27	40

For each pair of values, _x_ and _y_:

$$\frac{\$20}{2\,h} = \underline{\quad 10 \quad} \qquad \frac{\$27}{3\,h} = \underline{\quad 9 \quad} \qquad \frac{\$40}{4\,h} = \underline{\quad 10 \quad}$$

Because the amount of money Daniel earns is _not constant_, _x_ and _y_ are _not in direct proportion_.

Name: _____   Date: _____

Complete.

12. The table shows the amount of time, y hours, needed to service x cars at a garage.

Number of Cars (x)	2	3	4
Time (y hours)	14	21	28

For each pair of values, x and y:

$\dfrac{14 \text{ h}}{2 \text{ cars}} =$ _____ $\dfrac{21 \text{ h}}{3 \text{ cars}} =$ _____ $\dfrac{28 \text{ h}}{4 \text{ cars}} =$ _____

Is the time taken to service each car directly proportional to the number

of cars? _____

If so, what is the constant of proportionality? _____

What does this value represent? _____

Write the direct proportion equation. _____

Tell whether y is directly proportional to x. If so, find the constant of proportionality and write the direct proportion equation.

13. The table below shows the time taken, y hours, to paint the interior of x apartments.

Number of Apartments (x)	2	3	4
Time (y hours)	18	27	36

14. The table below shows the cost, y dollars, of x melons.

Number of Melons (x)	2	4	6
Cost (y dollars)	10	20	30

Tell whether each equation represents a direct proportion. If so, identify the constant of proportionality.

> *Example*
>
> $2m = 5n$
>
> $2m = 5n$
>
> $\dfrac{1}{2} \cdot 2m = 5n \cdot \dfrac{1}{2}$ Multiply both sides by $\dfrac{1}{2}$.
>
> $m = \dfrac{5}{2}n$ Simplify.
>
> Can the original equation $2m = 5n$ be written as an equivalent
>
> equation $m = \mathbf{k}n$? ___Yes___
>
> Is the equation a direct proportion, and if so, what is the constant
> of proportionality?
>
> Yes, it represents a direct proportion. The constant of proportionality is $\dfrac{5}{2}$.

Try to rewrite the equation as an equivalent equation in the form $y = kx$.

15. $3m = 5n$

$3m = 5n$

$\dfrac{1}{\boxed{}} \cdot 3m = 5n \cdot \dfrac{1}{\boxed{}}$ Divide both sides by _____.

$m = $ _____

Can the original equation $3m = 5n$ be written as an equivalent equation

$m = \mathbf{k}n$? _____

Is the equation a direct proportion, and if so, what is the constant of proportionality?

_____

16. $0.5y = x$ **17.** $4y = x + 1$

Name: _____   Date: _____

Find the constant of proportionality and tell what it represents in each situation. Then, write the direct proportion equation.

Example

The table shows the number of potatoes, y, baked in x hours. y is directly proportional to x. Find the constant of proportionality and tell what it represents in this situation. Then write a direct proportional equation.

Time (*x* hours)	2	3	5
Number of Potatoes (*y*)	80	120	200

Constant of proportionality: $\dfrac{80 \text{ potatoes}}{2 \text{ h}} = 40$

The constant of proportionality is ___40___ and represents *the number of potatoes*

baked per hour ___.

The direct proportion equation is _y = 40x_.

Complete.

18. The table below shows the number of points scored, *P*, in *m* basketball games. *P* is directly proportional to *m*. Find the constant of proportionality and tell what it represents in this situation. Then write a direct proportion equation.

Number of Games (*m*)	2	3	5
Number of Points (*P*)	26	39	65

Constant of proportionality: $\dfrac{\boxed{} \text{ points}}{\boxed{} \text{ games}} = $ _____

The constant of proportionality is _____ and represents _____

_____ .

The direct proportion equation is _____ .

Name: _____   Date: _____

Find the constant of proportionality and tell what it represents in each situation. Then, write the direct proportion equation.

19. The table shows the number of books, B, sold in a bookstore in t hours. B is directly proportional to t. Find the constant of proportionality and tell what it represents in this situation. Then write a direct proportion equation.

Time (t hours)	2	4	7
Numbers of Books (B)	10	20	35

20. Felicia uses a table to record the number of red cars, R, that passed by her house in t hours. R is directly proportional to t. Find the constant of proportionality and state what it represents in this situation. Then write a direct proportion equation.

Time (t hours)	4	12	20
Numbers of Red Cars (R)	3	9	15

21. Benny records the distance, D meters, he traveled on a bicycle in x minutes. D is directly proportional to x. Find the constant of proportionality and tell what it represents in this situation. Then write a direct proportional equation.

Time (x minutes)	2	5	30
Distance (D meters)	120	300	1,800

Lesson 5.2   Representing Direct Proportion Graphically

Tell whether each graph represents a direct proportion. If so, find the constant of proportionality. Then write a direct proportion equation.

Example

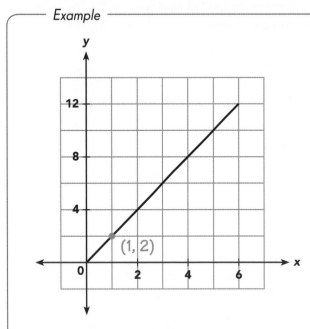

You can use (1, 2) to find the constant of proportionality.

Is the graph a straight line that passes through the origin? __Yes__

So, does the graph represent a direct proportion? __Yes__

Because the graph passes through (__1__, __2__), the constant of proportionality is __2__.

The direct proportion equation is _y = 2x_.

Complete.

1.

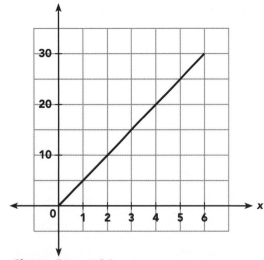

Is the graph a straight line that passes through the origin?_____

So, does the graph represent a direct proportion? _____

Because the graph passes through the point (_____, _____), the constant of proportionality is _____.

The direct proportion equation is _____.

Tell whether each graph represents a direct proportion. If so, find the constant of proportionality. Then write a direct proportion equation.

2.

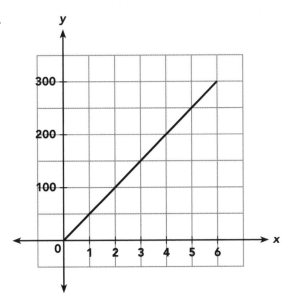

3.

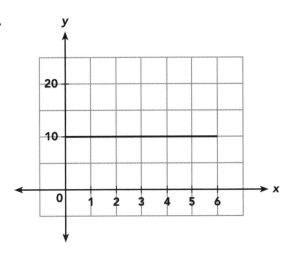

4.

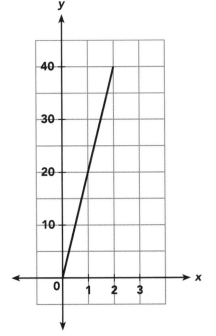

5.

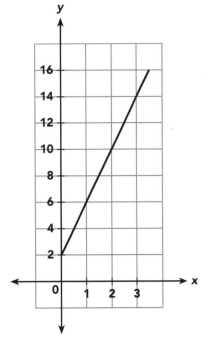

Name: _____   Date: _____

Interpret a graph of direct proportion.

Example

Shawn is a mechanic. The number of cars he services is directly proportional to the number of hours he works. The graph shows the number of cars, N, serviced in t hours.

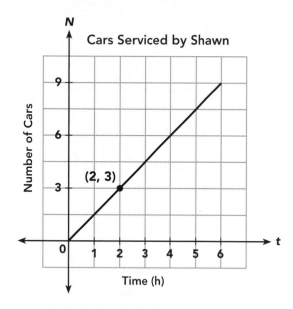

a) Find the constant of proportionality. What is the number of cars Shawn serviced per hour?

Constant of proportionality: $\dfrac{3}{2} = 1.5$

The constant of proportionality is ___1.5___. So, Shawn services ___1.5___ cars per hour.

b) Write a direct proportion equation.

The direct proportion equation is $\underline{N = 1.5t}$.

c) Explain what the point (2, 3) represents in this situation.

It means that Shawn services ___3___ cars in ___2___ hours.

d) If Shawn works 6 hours, how many cars can he service?

From the graph, Shawn can service ___9___ cars in ___6___ hours.

e) If Shawn wants to service 6 cars, how many hours should he plan to work?

From the graph, it will take Shawn ___4___ hours to service 6 cars.

Name: _____   Date: _____

Complete.

6. Jack services air-conditioners in a building. The number of air-conditioners he services is directly proportional to the number of hours he works. The graph shows the number of air-conditioners, A, serviced in t hours.

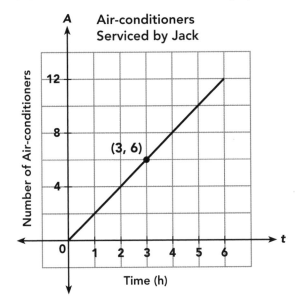

a) Find the constant of proportionality. What is the number of air conditioners Jack services per hour?

Constant of proportionality: _____ = _____

The constant of proportionality is _____. So, Jack serviced _____ air-conditioners per hour.

b) Write a direct proportion equation.

The direct proportion equation is _____.

c) Explain what the point (3, 6) represents in this situation.

It means that Jack services _____ air-conditioners in _____ hours.

d) Find the number of air-conditioners serviced in 6 hours.

From the graph, the number of air-conditioners serviced is _____.

e) How long does it take Jack to service 8 air-conditioners?

From the graph, it takes him _____ hours to service 8 air-conditioners.

Name: _____   Date: _____

Solve.

7. Cheryl works as a hotel maid. The number of hotel rooms she cleans is directly proportional to the number of hours she works. The graph shows that R rooms are cleaned in t hours.

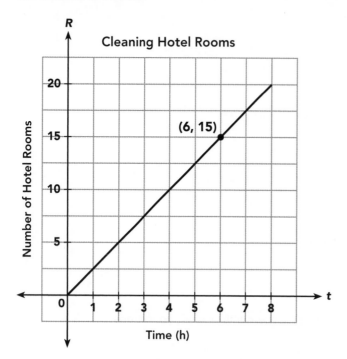

a) Find the constant of proportionality. What is the number of rooms Cheryl cleaned per hour?

b) Write a direct proportion equation.

c) Explain what the point (6, 15) represents in this situation.

d) Find the number of rooms that Cheryl can clean in 8 hours.

e) How many hours does it take Cheryl to clean 10 rooms?

Name: _____   Date: _____

Solve.

8. The number of tennis balls produced by a manufacturer is directly proportional to the number of hours the production line is operational. The graph shows the number of tennis balls, B, produced in t hours.

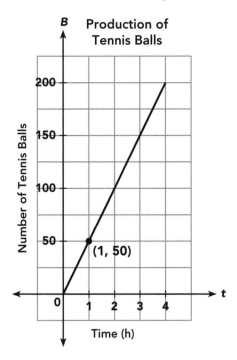

a) Find the constant of proportionality. What is the number of tennis balls produced per hour?

b) Write a direct proportion equation.

c) Explain what the point (1, 50) represents in this situation.

d) Find the number of tennis balls produced in 4 hours.

e) How many hours does it take to produce 100 tennis balls?

Lesson 5.3   Solving Direct Proportion Problems

Write a direct variation equation and find the indicated value.

Example

y varies directly as x, and $y = 6$ when $x = 2$.

a)   Write an equation that relates y and x.

Constant of proportionality: $\dfrac{y}{x} = \dfrac{6}{2} = 3$

The direct proportion equation is _$y = 3x$_.

Since y is directly proportional to x, you can use $\dfrac{y}{x} = k$ to find the constant of proportionality.

b)   Find y when $x = 6$.

Method 1
Use a proportion.

$$\dfrac{6}{2} = \dfrac{y}{6}$$

$$2 \cdot y = 6 \cdot 6$$

$$2y = 36$$

$$\dfrac{2y}{2} = \dfrac{36}{2}$$

$$y = 18$$

Method 2
Use a direction proportion equation.

When $x =$ ___6___ and $y =$ ___3x___,

$$y = 3 \cdot 6$$

$$y = 18$$

c)   Find x when $y = 24$.

Method 1
Use a proportion.

$$\dfrac{6}{2} = \dfrac{24}{x}$$

$$6 \cdot x = 24 \cdot 2$$

$$6x = 48$$

$$\dfrac{6x}{6} = \dfrac{48}{6}$$

$$x = 8$$

Method 2
Use a direction proportion equation.

When $y =$ ___24___ and $y =$ ___3x___,

$$24 = 3x$$

$$\dfrac{24}{3} = \dfrac{3x}{3}$$

$$8 = x$$

Name: _____ Date: _____

Complete.

1. p varies directly as r, and $p = 12$ when $r = 3$.

a) Write an equation that relates p and r.

Constant of proportionality: $\frac{p}{r} = $ _____ $= $ _____

The direct proportion equation is $p = $ _____ r.

b) Find p when $r = 4$.

Method 1
Use a proportion.

$$\frac{12}{3} = \frac{p}{\boxed{}}$$

$p \cdot 3 = 12 \cdot$ _____

$3p = $ _____

_____ $= $ _____

$p = $ _____

Method 2
Use a direction proportion equation.

When $r = 4$ and $p = $ _____ r,

$p = $ _____ $\cdot$ _____

$p = $ _____

c) Find r when $p = 40$.

Method 1
Use a proportion.

$$\frac{12}{3} = \frac{\boxed{}}{r}$$

$12 \cdot r = $ _____ $\cdot$ _____

$12r = $ _____

_____ $= $ _____

$r = $ _____

Method 2
Use a direction proportion equation.

When $p = 40$ and $p = $ _____ r,

$40 = $ _____

_____ $= $ _____

_____ $= r$

Name: _____ Date: _____

Write a direct variation equation and find the indicated value.

2. *m* varies directly as *n*, and *m* = 18 when *n* = 6.

    a) Write an equation that relates *m* and *n*.

    b) Find *m* when *n* = 3.

    c) Find *n* when *m* = 36.

3. *y* varies directly as *x*, and *y* = 5 when *x* = 10

    a) Write an equation that relates *y* and *x*.

    b) Find *y* when *x* = 8.

    c) Find *x* when *y* = 25.

4. *s* varies directly as *q*, and *s* = 2 when *q* = 5.

    a) Write an equation that relates *s* and *q*.

    b) Find *s* when *q* = 25.

    c) Find *q* when *s* = 8.

Name: _____   Date: _____

In each table, *y* is directly proportional to *x*. Complete the table.

Example

	2	a) _____	5
x	2	a) _____	5
y	10	15	b) _____

a) $\dfrac{10}{2} = \dfrac{15}{x}$

$x \cdot 10 = 2 \cdot 15$

$10x = 30$

$\dfrac{10x}{10} = \dfrac{30}{10}$

$x = 3$

Since *y* is directly proportional to *x*, you can use proportional reasoning to solve for the unknown values.

b) $\dfrac{10}{2} = \dfrac{y}{5}$

$5 \cdot 10 = 2 \cdot y$

$50 = 2y$

$\dfrac{50}{2} = \dfrac{2y}{2}$

$25 = y$

Complete.

5.

x	4	a) _____	10
y	12	18	b) _____

a) $\dfrac{12}{4} = \dfrac{\boxed{}}{x}$

$x \cdot 12 = 4 \cdot$ _____

$12x =$ _____

_____ $=$ _____

$x =$ _____

b) $\dfrac{12}{4} = \dfrac{\boxed{}}{10}$

$12 \cdot$ _____ $=$ _____ $\cdot 4$

_____ $= 4y$

_____ $=$ _____

_____ $= y$

In each table, *y* is directly proportional to *x*. Complete the table.

6.

x	2	a) _____	5
y	14	28	b) _____

7.

x	4	a) _____	16
y	1	3	b) _____

8.

x	3	a) _____	7
y	42	70	b) _____

Solve a real-world direct proportion problem.

Example

The mass of a collection of copper coins, y grams, is directly proportional to the
number of coins in the collection, c. The mass of 12 coins is 36 grams.

a) Find the constant of proportionality.

Constant of proportionality: $\dfrac{y}{c} = \dfrac{36}{12} = 3$

The constant of proportionality is ___3___.

b) Write an equation that relates y and c.

The direct proportion equation is _y = 3c_.

c) Find the mass of a collection of 30 coins.

When c = __30__ and y = __3c__, y = _3 · 30_

y = __90__

The mass of a collection of 30 coins is __90__ grams.

Complete.

9. The number of tourists, n, in a tour group, is directly proportional to the number
of buses, c, a travel agent needs to reserve. A travel agent reserves 6 buses for
360 tourists.

a) Find the constant of proportionality.

Constant of proportionality: $\dfrac{n}{c} =$ _____ = _____

The constant of proportionality is _____.

b) Write an equation that relates c to n.

The direct proportion equation is _____.

c) Find the value of c when n = 240.

When n = _____ and n = _____c, _____ = _____ · c

_____ = _____

_____ = c

Name: _____   Date: _____

Solve. Show your work.

10. The number of cell phones produced by a manufacturer, *s*, is directly proportional to the number of hours, *h*, that the production line is operational. The production line is capable of producing 72 cell phones in 48 hours.

   a) Find the constant of proportionality.

   b) Write an equation that relates *s* and *h*.

   c) Find the value of *s* when *h* = 40.

11. The number of loaves of bread, *N*, produced at a local bakery is directly proportional to the time it takes to bake the bread, *T*. It takes 4 hours to bake 220 loaves of bread.

   a) Find the number of loaves of bread baked in 1 hour.

   b) Write an equation that relates *N* and *T*.

   c) How long does it take to bake 330 loaves of bread?

12. The distance traveled by an aircraft, *d* miles, is directly proportional to the duration of the flight, *t* hours. It takes 3 hours to travel 1,350 miles.

   a) Find the distance the aircraft travels in 1 hour.

   b) Write an equation that relates *d* and *t*.

   c) How long does it take to travel 2,250 miles?

Solve. Show your work.

Example

For every $150 that Susan earns, she donates $20 to a charity. Last month, Susan donated $32 to a charity. How much did she earn last month?

Method 1
Use a proportion.

Let y be the amount she earned.   Define the variable.

$$\frac{150 \text{ dollars}}{20 \text{ dollars}} = \frac{y \text{ dollars}}{32 \text{ dollars}}$$ Write a proportion.

$$\frac{150}{20} = \frac{y}{32}$$ Write ratios as fractions.

$y \cdot 20 = 150 \cdot 32$ Write cross products.

$20y = 4{,}800$ Simplify.

$$\frac{20y}{20} = \frac{4{,}800}{20}$$ Divide both sides by 20.

$y = 240$ Simplify.

Susan earned __$240__ last month.

Method 2
Use a direct proportion equation.

Let x be the amount she donated to the   Define the variables.
charity. Let y be the amount she earns.

Constant of proportionality:

$$\frac{y}{x} = \frac{150}{20}$$ Substitute $y = 150$ and $x = 20$.

$= 7.5$ Simplify.

Direct proportion equation: $y = 7.5x$

When $x = $ __32__ and $y = $ __7.5x__ , $y = 7.5 \cdot 32$

$y = $ __240__

Susan earned __$240__ last month.

Complete.

13. For every 200 microchips produced in a factory, there are 8 defective microchips. If there were 33 defective microchips, how many microchips did the factory produce?

Method 1
Use a proportion.

Let y be the number of microchips produced.　　　Define the variables.

$$\frac{\boxed{} \text{ microchips}}{8 \text{ defective}} = \frac{y \text{ microchips}}{\boxed{} \text{ defective}}$$　　Write a proportion.

$$\frac{\boxed{}}{8} = \frac{y}{\boxed{}}$$　　Write ratios as fractions.

$$y \cdot 8 = \underline{\hspace{1.5cm}} \cdot \underline{\hspace{1.5cm}}$$　　Write cross products.

$$8y = \underline{\hspace{1.5cm}}$$　　Simplify.

$$\underline{\hspace{1.5cm}} = \underline{\hspace{1.5cm}}$$　　Divide both sides by _____.

$$y = \underline{\hspace{1.5cm}}$$　　Simplify.

The factory produced _____ microchips.

Method 2
Use a direct proportion equation.

Let x be the number of defective microchips.　　Define the variables.
Let y be the number of microchips produced.

Constant of proportionality:

$$\frac{y}{x} = \underline{\hspace{1.5cm}}$$
　　　　　　　　　　　　　Substitute $y = $ _____ and $x = $ _____.

$$= \underline{\hspace{1.5cm}}$$　　Simplify.

Direct proportion equation: $y = $ _____

When $x = $ _____ and $y = $ _____, $y = $ _____ · _____

$$y = \underline{\hspace{1.5cm}}$$

The factory produced _____ microchips.

Solve. Show your work.

14. In a particular country, a value added tax of $5 is levied on every $100 worth of goods sold. Shirley wants to buy a piece of luggage that costs $360. How much value added tax must she pay?

15. There are 243 milligrams of calcium in 54 grams of an energy drink powder. Gabe used 30 grams of energy drink powder to make a drink. How many milligrams of calcium did the drink contain?

16. A 12-ounce avocado contains 20 milligrams of vitamin C. An avocado salad uses 60 ounces of avocados. How much vitamin C do the avocados contribute to the salad?

Solve a direct proportion problem involving percent.

___ *Example* ___

Last year, 250 students attended a band camp. This year, 50 more students attended the band camp than last year. Use a proportion to find the percent increase in the number of students who attended the band camp this year.

Method 1
Use a proportion.

Let x be the percent increase in the number of students who attended the band camp.

$$\frac{100 \text{ percent}}{250 \text{ students}} = \frac{x \text{ percent}}{50 \text{ students}}$$ 　　　　Write a proportion.

$$\frac{100}{250} = \frac{x}{50}$$ 　　　　Write ratios as fractions.

$$x \cdot 250 = 100 \cdot 50$$ 　　　　Write cross products.

$$250x = 5,000$$ 　　　　Simplify.

$$\frac{250x}{250} = \frac{5,000}{250}$$ 　　　　Divide both sides by 250.

$$x = 20$$ 　　　　Simplify.

The percent increase in the number of students who attended the band camp this year is __20%__.

Method 2
Use a ratio.

Ratio of percents = Ratio of number of students
x percent : 100 percent = 50 : 250 　　　　Write a proportion.

$$\frac{x}{100} = \frac{50}{250}$$ 　　　　Write ratios as fractions.

$$100 \cdot \frac{x}{100} = \frac{50}{250} \cdot 100$$ 　　　　Multiply both sides by 100.

$$x = 20$$ 　　　　Simplify.

The percent increase in the number of students who attended the band camp this year is __20%__.

Complete.

17. Brandon sold 180 pairs of shoes in June. He sold 45 fewer pairs of shoes in July than in June. What was the percent decrease in the number of pairs of shoes Brandon sold?

Method 1
Use a proportion.

Let x be the percentage decrease in the number of pairs of shoes Brandon sold.

$\dfrac{100 \text{ percent}}{180 \text{ pairs of shoes}} = \dfrac{x \text{ percent}}{\boxed{} \text{ pairs of shoes}}$ Write a proportion.

$\dfrac{100}{180} = \dfrac{x}{\boxed{}}$ Write ratios as fractions.

$x \cdot 180 = 100 \cdot \underline{\hspace{2cm}}$ Write cross products.

$180x = \underline{\hspace{2cm}}$ Simplify.

$\dfrac{180x}{\boxed{}} = \underline{\hspace{2cm}}$ Divide both sides by _____.

$x = \underline{\hspace{2cm}}$ Simplify.

The percent decrease in the number of pairs of shoes Brandon sold is _____.

Method 2
Use a ratio.

Ratio of percents = Ratio of number of pairs of shoes sold

$x \text{ percent} : 100 \text{ percent} = \underline{\hspace{2cm}} : \underline{\hspace{2cm}}$ Write a proportion.

$\dfrac{x}{100} = \underline{\hspace{2cm}}$ Write ratios as fractions.

$100 \cdot \dfrac{x}{100} = \underline{\hspace{2cm}} \cdot 100$ Multiply both sides by 100.

$x = \underline{\hspace{2cm}}$ Simplify.

The percent decrease in the number of pairs of shoes Brandon sold is _____.

Use a proportion to solve each question. Show your work.

18. Austin's monthly salary was $1,500. At the end of the year, he was promoted and received a raise of $300. Find the percent increase in his salary.

19. In 2008, about 47 million tourists visited New York City. In 2009, New York City had about 1.4 million fewer tourists. Find the percent decrease in the number of tourists who visited New York City. Give your answer to the nearest percent.

20. In 2000, the state of Texas had a population of about 20.85 million. By 2010, the population had grown by 4.3 million. What is the percent increase in the population of the state of Texas? Give your answer to the nearest percent.

Lesson 5.4 Understanding Inverse Proportion

Tell whether two quantities are in inverse proportion from a table. If so, find the constant of proportionality.

Example

x	2	4	6
y	12	6	4

For each pair of values, x and y:

$xy = 2 \cdot 12$ $xy = 4 \cdot 6$ $xy = 6 \cdot 4$
$\quad = 24$ $\quad = 24$ $\quad = 24$

Check to see whether the product of x and y is a constant value.

Is x inversely proportional to y? ___Yes___

If yes, what is the constant of proportionality?___24___

Complete.

1.

x	2	3	6
y	18	12	6

For each pair of values, x and y:

$2 \cdot 18 =$ _____   _____ $\cdot 12 =$ _____   _____ $\cdot$ _____ $=$ _____

Is x inversely proportional to y? _____

If yes, what is the constant of proportionality? _____

2.

x	2	5	15
y	25	10	3

For each pair of values, x and y:

$2 \cdot 25 =$ _____ $5 \cdot$ _____ $=$ _____   _____ $\cdot$ _____ $=$ _____

Is x inversely proportional to y? _____

If yes, what is the constant of proportionality? _____

Tell whether two quantities are in inverse proportion. If so, find the constant of proportionality.

3.

x	2	3	4
y	9	6	4.5

Is x inversely proportional to y? _____

If yes, what is the constant of proportionality?_____

4.

x	30	40	60
y	10	8	5

Is x inversely proportional to y? _____

If yes, what is the constant of proportionality?_____

5.

x	2	3	4
y	1	$\frac{2}{3}$	$\frac{1}{2}$

Is x inversely proportional to y? _____

If yes, what is the constant of proportionality?_____

Tell whether the equation represents an inverse proportion. If so, find the constant of proportionality.

Example

$$\frac{2}{3}y = \frac{6}{x}$$

$$\frac{2}{3}y = \frac{6}{x}$$

$$\frac{2}{3}y \cdot \frac{3}{2} = \frac{6}{x} \cdot \frac{3}{2}$$

$$y = \frac{9}{x}$$

$$y \cdot x = \frac{9}{x} \cdot x$$

$$xy = 9$$

Rewrite the equation as an equivalent equation in the form

$$xy = k \text{ or } y = \frac{k}{x}.$$

Can the original equation be written as two equivalent equations in the form

$xy = k$ and $y = \frac{k}{x}$? ___Yes___

Is the equation an inverse proportion, and if so, what is the constant of proportionality?

___Yes. The constant of proportionality is 9.___

Complete.

6. $3y = \frac{9}{x}$

$$3y = \frac{9}{x}$$

$$3y \cdot \text{_____} = \frac{9}{x} \cdot \text{_____}$$

$$y = \frac{\boxed{}}{x}$$

$$y \cdot x = \text{\_\_\_\_\_} \cdot x$$

$$xy = \text{_____}$$

Can the original equation be written as two equivalent equations in the form

$xy = k$ and $y = \frac{k}{x}$? _____

Is the equation an inverse proportion, and if so, what is the constant of proportionality?

_____

Name: _____   Date: _____

Complete.

7. $y + 6x = 8$

$$y + 6x = 8$$

$$y + 6x - \underline{\hspace{1.5cm}} = 8 - \underline{\hspace{1.5cm}}$$

$$\underline{\hspace{1.5cm}} = \underline{\hspace{1.5cm}} - \underline{\hspace{1.5cm}}$$

Can the original equation be written as two equivalent equations in the form
$xy = k$ and $y = \dfrac{k}{x}$? _____

Is the equation an inverse proportion, and if so, what is the constant of proportionality?

_____

Tell whether each equation represents an inverse proportion. If so, find the constant of proportionality.

8. $2y = \dfrac{4}{x}$

9. $3y = \dfrac{x}{9}$

10. $6x = \dfrac{2}{y}$

Name: _____   Date: _____

Each graph represents an inverse proportion. Find the constant of proportionality.

Example

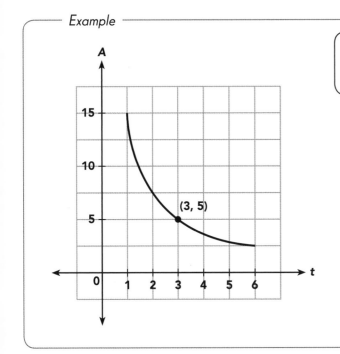

You can use the coordinates of any point (x, y) to find the constant of proportionality.

Constant of proportionality:

$(3, 5) \rightarrow$ ___3___ · ___5___ = ___15___

The constant of proportionality is ___15___.

Complete.

11.

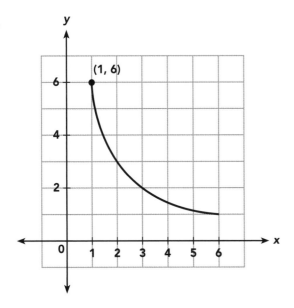

Constant of proportionality:

$(1, 6) \rightarrow$ _____ · _____ = _____

The constant of proportionality is _____.

Each graph represents an inverse proportion. Find the constant of proportionality.

12.

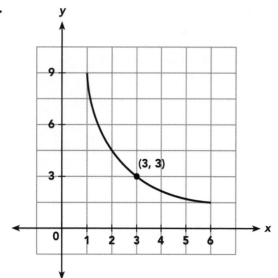

13.

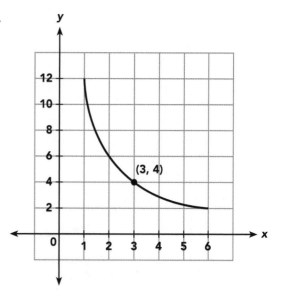

14.

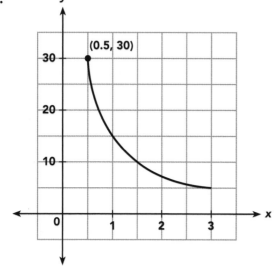

15.

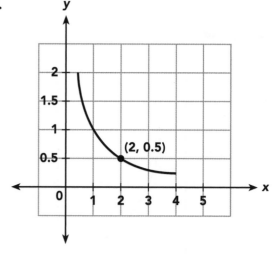

Name: _____   Date: _____

Solve an inverse proportion problem graphically.

Example

A school is holding a career fair in the school auditorium. The time it takes to set up the booths in the school auditorium is inversely proportional to the number of students helping to set up. The graph shows the amount of time, *t* hours, that it takes *n* students to set up the booths in the school auditorium.

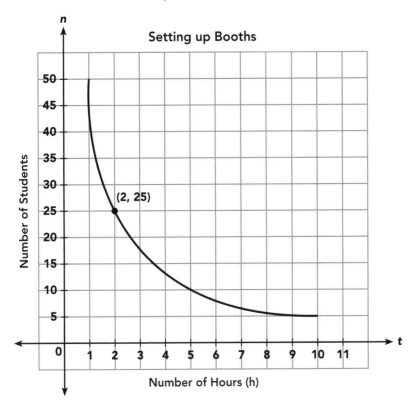

a) Find the constant of proportionality graphically. Then write an inverse proportion equation.

Use (2, 25) to find the constant of proportionality:

$t \cdot n = 2 \cdot 25$ Choose the point (2, 25).

$= 50$ Multiply.

You can choose any point (*x*, *y*) on the graph to find the constant of proportionality.

The constant of proportionality is ___50___.

The inverse proportion equation is *tn* = 50.

b) Explain what the point (2, 25) represents in this situation.

It means that it takes ___25___ students ___2___ hours to set up the booths in the school auditorium.

Name: _____   Date: _____

Complete.

16. The amount of time, t hours, it takes to fill a swimming pool with water is inversely proportional to the number of pipes, n, used to pump water into the swimming pool. The graph shows the relationship between t and n.

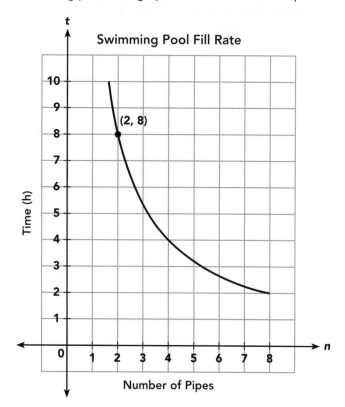

a) Find the constant of proportionality from the graph. Then write an inverse proportion equation.

Use (_____, _____) to find the constant of proportionality:

$n \cdot t = $ _____ · _____   Choose the point (_____, _____).

$= $ _____   Multiply.

The constant of proportionality is _____.

The inverse proportion equation is _____.

b) Explain what the point (2, 8) represents in this situation.

It means that _____ pipes can fill the swimming pool in _____ hours.

Name: _____   Date: _____

Solve an inverse proportion problem graphically.

17. The air pressure inside a weather balloon, P newton per square meter, is
inversely proportional to the volume of gas, V cubic meters, inside the balloon.
The graph shows the relationship between P and V.

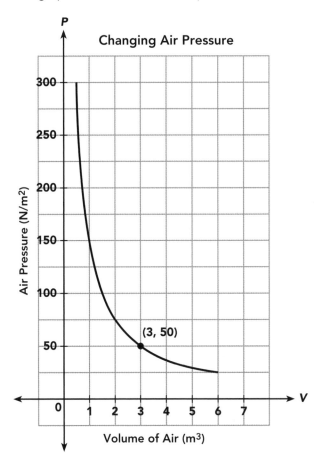

a) Find the constant of proportionality graphically. Then write an inverse
proportion equation.

b) Explain what the point (3, 50) represents in this situation.

Solve an inverse proportion problem graphically.

18. Sophie has a long piece of rope. She needs to cut the rope into shorter pieces. The number of shorter pieces Sophie cuts, n, is inversely proportional to the length, s meters, of each of the shorter pieces of rope. The graph shows the relationship between s and n.

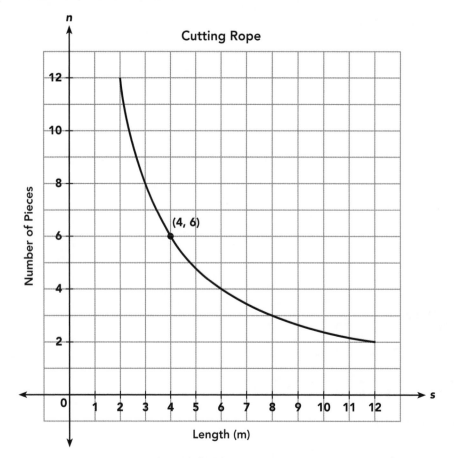

Cutting Rope

a) Find the constant of proportionality graphically. Then write an inverse proportion equation.

b) Explain what the point (4, 6) represents in this situation.

Answers

Chapter 1

Lesson 1.1

1. $0.4 < 0.9 < 1\frac{1}{2} < \frac{10}{3}$

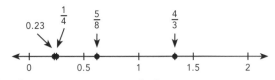

2. $0.23 < \frac{1}{4} < \frac{5}{8} < \frac{4}{3}$

3. $<$ **4.** $>$

5. 2,550   **6.** 23.2

7. 7,363.92   **8.** 7,364

9. 49; 343   **10.** 100; 1,000

11. 6   **12.** 9

13. 5   **14.** 8

15. $3^3 > \sqrt{100} > 2^2$

16. $4^2 > 2^3 > \sqrt{16}$

17. $=$ **18.** $<$

19. a) $\left|2\frac{2}{3}\right| = 2\frac{2}{3}$ and $\left|-\frac{9}{4}\right| = \frac{9}{4}$

b)

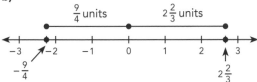

$2\frac{2}{3}$ is farther from 0.

20. a) $\frac{5}{8}; \frac{2}{3}$

b)

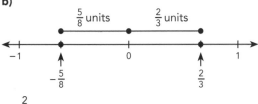

$\frac{2}{3}$

21. a) $1\frac{1}{4}; \frac{11}{6}$

b)

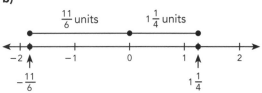

22. $3\frac{4}{6} = \dfrac{\boxed{6} \cdot \boxed{3}}{6} + \dfrac{\boxed{4}}{6} = \dfrac{22}{6} = \dfrac{11}{3}$

23. $-17 = \dfrac{-\boxed{17}}{1}$ or $= \dfrac{\boxed{17}}{-1}$

24. $-\dfrac{3}{2}$ **25.** $\dfrac{5}{3}$

26. $-\dfrac{14}{3}$ **27.** $\dfrac{10}{7}$

28. $7.5 = \boxed{7}\,\dfrac{\boxed{1}}{\boxed{2}}$

$= \dfrac{15}{2}$

29. $-\dfrac{3}{8}$ **30.** $\dfrac{18}{5}$

31. $-\dfrac{234}{25}$ **32.** $\dfrac{29}{8}$

33. $\dfrac{321}{100}$ **34.** $-\dfrac{209}{200}$

35. Step 1

$-\dfrac{1}{5}$ is a negative proper fraction so it is located between $\underline{-1}$ and $\underline{0}$.

$\dfrac{10}{4}$ can be written as a mixed number, $2\dfrac{1}{2}$, and $2\dfrac{1}{2}$, lies between $\underline{2}$ and $\underline{3}$.

Step 2

Step 3

You divide the distance between -1 and 0 into $\underline{5}$ equal segments and the distance between 2 and 3 into $\underline{2}$ equal segments.

Step 4

36.

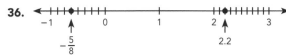

Lesson 1.2

1.

$$25\overline{)3.00}$$
$$\underline{25}$$
$$50$$
$$\underline{50}$$
$$0$$

(quotient 0.12)

$$\frac{3}{25} = 0.12$$

2.

$$16\overline{)17.0000}$$
$$\underline{16}$$
$$100$$
$$\underline{96}$$
$$40$$
$$\underline{32}$$
$$80$$
$$\underline{80}$$
$$0$$

(quotient 1.0625)

$$\frac{17}{16} = 1.0625$$

3. 2.125   **4.** 0.45

5. 0.1875   **6.** 2.25

7.

$$11\overline{)6.0000}$$
$$\underline{55}$$
$$50$$
$$\underline{44}$$
$$60$$
$$\underline{55}$$
$$50$$
$$\underline{44}$$
$$6$$

(quotient 0.5454)

$$\frac{6}{11} = 0.5454\ldots$$

8. From the calculator,

$$\frac{17}{15} = 1.1333\ldots$$

9. $0.\overline{2}$ **10.** $1.\overline{36}$

11. $2.16\overline{6}$ **12.** $1.0\overline{30}$

13. $1.\overline{63}$ **14.** $0.2\overline{7}$

15. $0.47\overline{2}$ **16.** $1.\overline{074}$

17. $\frac{22}{7} = 3.142857\ldots$

$$\frac{25}{8} = 3.125$$

Compare the decimals,
<u>3.142857...</u> and <u>3.125</u>.

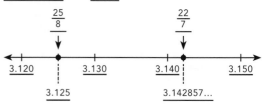

<u>3.142857...</u> lies to the right of <u>3.125</u>
or <u>3.142857...</u> > <u>3.125</u>.

So, $\frac{22}{7} > \frac{25}{8}$.

18.

$$\frac{3}{4} < \frac{5}{6}$$

19.

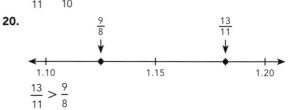

$$\frac{10}{11} > \frac{9}{10}$$

20.

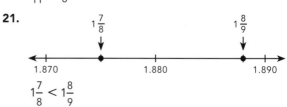

$$\frac{13}{11} > \frac{9}{8}$$

21.

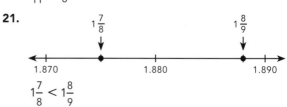

$$1\frac{7}{8} < 1\frac{8}{9}$$

22. *Method 1*

Compare using a number line.

$-2\frac{7}{8} = \underline{-2.875}$

$|-2.875| = \underline{2.875}$

$-2\frac{8}{9} = \underline{-2.888...} = \underline{-2.\overline{8}}$

$|-2.\overline{8}| = \underline{2.\overline{8}}$

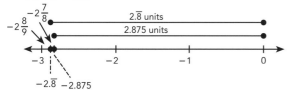

From the number line, you see that $\underline{-2.\overline{8}}$ lies farther to the left of 0 than $\underline{-2.875}$ or $\underline{-2.875} > \underline{-2.\overline{8}}$.

So, $-2\frac{7}{8} \underline{>} -2\frac{8}{9}$.

Method 2

Compare using place value

$|-2.875| \underline{<} |-2.\overline{8}|$

The number with the greater absolute value is $\underline{-2.\overline{8}}$ and it is farther to the left of 0. Hence it is the $\underline{\text{lesser}}$ number. So, $\underline{-2.875} > \underline{-2.8}$.

So, $-2\frac{7}{8} \underline{>} -2\frac{8}{9}$.

23. $-\frac{3}{4} \underline{>} -\frac{4}{5}$ **24.** $-\frac{22}{7} \underline{<} -3\frac{1}{10}$

Lesson 1.3

1. $\sqrt{4}$, 5, $\frac{1}{9}$, $\left(\sqrt{2}\right)$, -2.31, $\left(\sqrt{7}\right)$

2. $-\frac{19}{11}$, $\left(-\sqrt{23}\right)$, 13, $\left(\sqrt{8}\right)$, 3.001

3. Which two whole numbers is $\sqrt{14}$ between? $\underline{3}$ and $\underline{4}$
Find an approximate value of $\sqrt{14}$ by using a calculator: $\sqrt{14} = \underline{3.741657387...}$
$\sqrt{14}$ lies between the tenths $\underline{3.7}$ and $\underline{3.8}$.
The value of $\sqrt{14}$ with 2 decimal places is $\underline{3.74}$.
Which tenth is $\sqrt{14}$ closer to? $\underline{3.7}$

4. 2; 3

5. 2; 3

6. 4; 5

7. 5; 6

8. Which two integers is $-\sqrt{8}$ between? $\underline{-2}$ and $\underline{-3}$
Find an approximate value of $-\sqrt{8}$ by using a calculator:
$-\sqrt{8} = \underline{-2.828427125...}$
$-\sqrt{8}$ lies between the tenths $\underline{-2.8}$ and $\underline{-2.9}$.
The value of $-\sqrt{8}$ with 2 decimal places is $\underline{-2.83}$.
Which tenth is $-\sqrt{8}$ closer to? $\underline{-2.8}$

9. -2; -3

10. -4; -5

11. -5; -6

12. -6; -7

13. 7.280

14. -10.817

Lesson 1.4

1. $<$ **2.** $>$

3. $<$ **4.** $<$

5. Use a calculator to represent each number in decimal form with 3 decimal places.

$0.\overline{831} \approx \underline{0.832}$, $-\sqrt{8} \approx \underline{-2.828}$,

$\frac{p}{2} \approx \underline{1.571}$, $\frac{1}{7} \approx \underline{0.143}$,

$-\sqrt{7} \approx \underline{-2.646}$

Ordering the numbers from least to greatest using the symbol $<$,

$\underline{-\sqrt{8}} < \underline{-\sqrt{7}} < \frac{1}{7} < \underline{0.831} < \frac{p}{2}$

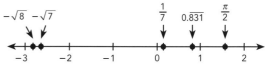

6. $\frac{10}{3} \approx 3.333$, $\sqrt{10} \approx 3.162$,

$\frac{2p}{3} \approx 2.094$, $\frac{3}{7} \approx 0.429$,

$\sqrt{3} \approx 1.732$

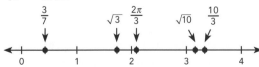

7. $-\sqrt{7} \approx -2.646$, $-\frac{11}{3} \approx -3.667$,

$0.\overline{54} \approx 0.545$, $-\frac{\sqrt{5}}{2} \approx -1.118$,

$\frac{14}{15} \approx 0.933$

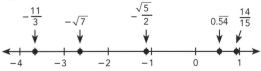

8. $\frac{158}{60} \approx 2.633$, $\sqrt{2} \approx 1.414$,

$\frac{p^2}{5} \approx 1.974$, $\frac{3}{13} \approx 0.231$,

$-0.84173 \approx -0.842$

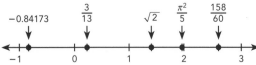

9. $-2.3\overline{84} \approx -2.385$, $-\frac{4}{17} \approx -0.235$,

$-\sqrt{15} \approx -3.873$, $-\frac{183}{58} \approx -3.155$,

$-\frac{\sqrt{99}}{8} \approx -1.244$

Lesson 1.5

1. <u>2, 3, 0, and 4</u> are significant digits.
There are <u>4</u> significant digits.

2. <u>2 and 1</u> are significant digits.
There are <u>2</u> significant digits.

3. <u>3 and 1</u> are significant digits.
There are <u>2</u> significant digits.

4. <u>4, 5, and 0</u> are significant digits.
There are <u>3</u> significant digits.

5. <u>6, 0, 2, and 3</u> are significant digits.
There are <u>4</u> significant digits.

6. <u>9, 0, and 1</u> are significant digits.
There are <u>3</u> significant digits.

7. <u>2, 1, 0, and 4</u> are significant digits.
There are <u>4</u> significant digits.

8. <u>1, 9, 6, and 9</u> are significant digits.
There are <u>4</u> significant digits.

9. <u>8 and 3</u> are significant digits.
There are <u>2</u> significant digits.

10. The 5th significant digit is <u>4</u>, which is <u>less than</u> 5.
128,043 is closer to <u>128,000</u> than to <u>128,100</u>.
So, the integer rounded to 4 significant digits is <u>128,000</u>.

11. The 6th significant digit is <u>9</u>, which is <u>greater than</u> 5.
150,659 is closer to <u>150,660</u> than to <u>150,650</u>.
So, the integer rounded to 5 significant digits is <u>150,660</u>.

12. The 3rd significant digit is <u>5</u>.
23,513 is exactly between <u>23,000</u> and <u>24,000</u>.
So, the integer rounded to 2 significant digits is <u>24,000</u>.

13. 290   **14.** 208,600

15. 8,860   **16.** 3,929,720

17. Only 4 significant digits are required. The 5th significant digit is <u>0</u>, which is <u>less than</u> 5.
So, the decimal rounded to 4 significant digits is <u>19.62</u>.

18. Only 5 significant digits are required. The 6th significant digit is <u>6</u>, which is <u>greater than</u> 5.
So, the decimal rounded to 5 significant digits is <u>232.16</u>.

19. Only 6 significant digits are required. The 7th significant digit is <u>5</u>, which is <u>exactly</u> 5.
So, the decimal rounded to 6 significant digits is <u>200.000</u>.

20. 35.4   **21.** 6.0239

22. 93.99010

23. **a)** Total mass = <u>8</u> · <u>12.256</u>
            = <u>98.048</u> g

     b) <u>98</u> g

24. 0.905 mm

Chapter 2

Lesson 2.1

1. >   **2.** >

3. <   **4.** <

5. 88   **6.** 69

7. $1\frac{3}{8}$ **8.** $3\frac{1}{3}$

9. $\frac{11}{3}$ **10.** $\frac{38}{7}$

11. $\frac{13}{14}$ **12.** $1\frac{11}{18}$

13. $\frac{3}{4}$ **14.** $\frac{1}{12}$

15. 9.15   **16.** 4.32

17. $42   **18.** 30

19. 20%

20. **a)** $464

     b) 80%

21. *Method 1*

Use a number line to model the sum of two negative integers.

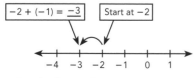

$-2 + (-1) = \underline{-3}$

Method 2

Use absolute values to find the sum of two negative integers.

$$|-2| = \underline{2}$$
$$|-1| = \underline{1}$$
$$|-2| + |-1| = \underline{2} + \underline{1}$$
$$= \underline{3}$$
$$-2 + (-1) = \underline{-3}$$

22. -9

23. -14

24. -18

25. -10

26. 0

27. 0

28. $|-14| = \underline{14}$ $|8| = \underline{8}$
$$|-14| - |8| = \underline{14} - \underline{8}$$
$$= \underline{6}$$
$$(-14) + 8 = \underline{-6}$$

29. -6

30. -11

31. $9 + (-5) + 8 = \underline{4} + 8$
$$= \underline{12}$$

32. $-6 + 2 + (-8) = -6 + \underline{(-8)} + 2$
$$= \underline{-14} + 2$$
$$= \underline{-12}$$

33. -5

34. -5

35. The helicopter rises 197 feet.

Lesson 2.2

1. $-250 - 180 = -250 + \underline{(-180)}$

Using absolute values,

$$|-250| + |\underline{-180}| = 250 + \underline{180}$$
$$= \underline{430}$$
$$-250 - 180 = -250 + \underline{(-180)}$$
$$= \underline{-430}$$

The submarine is $\underline{430}$ feet below sea level now.

2. -14

3. -12

4. $-21°C$

5. $22 - (-9) = 22 + \underline{9}$
$$= \underline{31}$$

6. $-17 - (-5) = -17 + \underline{5}$

Using absolute values,

$$|-17| - |-5| = \underline{17} - \underline{5}$$
$$= \underline{12}$$
$$-17 - (-5) = -17 + \underline{5}$$
$$= \underline{-12}$$

7. 23

8. -8

9. -9

10. -2

11. 31

12. 15

13. *Method 1*

Use a number line to plot the points and count the units.

5 units

The distance between 4 and -1 is $\underline{5}$ units.

Method 2

Use absolute values to find the distance between integers with opposite signs.

Distance between 4 and -1:

$$|4 - (-1)| = |\underline{4 + 1}|$$
$$= \underline{5}$$

14. 16 units

15. 26 units

16. Elevation of Jason: 54 ft

Elevation of David: $\underline{-11}$ ft

Difference between their elevations:

$$|54 - (\underline{-11})| = |\underline{54 + 11}|$$
$$= \underline{65} \text{ ft}$$

The difference in their elevations is $\underline{65}$ feet.

17. 3,035 ft

Lesson 2.3

1. -63

2. -36

3. 28

4. 25

5. 60

6. 70

7. Change in temperature = Rate · Time
$$= \underline{-2} \cdot \underline{9}$$
$$= \underline{-18}°C$$

The total change in temperature of the compound is $\underline{-18}°C$.

8. -24 points

9. -91 m

10. 8

11. -4

12. -4

13. 7

14. -25 ft/s

15. -54 m/s

Lesson 2.4

1. $20 + 6 - 2 \cdot 4 = 20 + 6 - \underline{8}$
$$= \underline{26} + \underline{(-8)}$$
$$= \underline{18}$$

2. $(-15 - 25) \div 8 - 12 = \underline{-40} \div 8 - 12$
$$= \underline{-5} - 12$$
$$= \underline{-17}$$

3. $-11 - (5 + 2) + 3 = -11 - \underline{7} + 3$

$$= -11 + \underline{(-7)} + 3$$
$$= \underline{-18} + 3$$
$$= \underline{-15}$$

4. -27 **5.** 9

6. -22 **7.** -29

8. Two-fifth of 100:

$(100 \div 5) \cdot 2 = \underline{40}$ sandwiches

$\underline{40}$ sandwiches sold at $1 each:

$\underline{40} \cdot \$1 = \underline{\$40}$

Number of sandwiches sold at three for $2:

$100 - \underline{40} = \underline{60}$ sandwiches

Number of sets of $\underline{60}$ sandwiches:

$\underline{60} \div 3 = \underline{20}$ sets

Cost of $\underline{20}$ sets of sandwiches:

$\underline{20} \cdot \$2 = \underline{\$40}$

Profit:

$\underline{\$40} + \underline{\$40} - \underline{\$60} = \underline{\$20}$

His profit is $\underline{\$20}$.

9. 74 in²   **10.** 68 in²

11. $40   **12.** $20

Lesson 2.5

1. $-1\frac{1}{2} + 2\frac{3}{8} = -1\frac{4}{8} + 2\frac{3}{8}$

$$= (-1 + 2) - \frac{4}{8} + \frac{3}{8}$$
$$= 1 + \left(\frac{-1}{8}\right)$$
$$= \frac{7}{8}$$

2. $\frac{1}{4} + \left(\frac{-5}{12}\right) + \left(\frac{-2}{3}\right) = \frac{1 \cdot 3}{4 \cdot 3} + \left(\frac{-5}{12}\right) + \frac{-2 \cdot 4}{3 \cdot 4}$

$$= \frac{3}{12} + \left(\frac{-5}{12}\right) + \left(\frac{-8}{12}\right)$$
$$= \frac{(3) + (-5) + (-8)}{12}$$
$$= \frac{-10}{12}$$
$$= -\frac{5}{6}$$

3. $-\frac{19}{20}$ **4.** $1\frac{1}{2}$

5. $-1\frac{1}{4}$ **6.** $\frac{1}{24}$

7. $\frac{1}{5} - \frac{2}{15} = \frac{1 \cdot 3}{5 \cdot 3} - \frac{2}{15}$

$$= \frac{3}{15} - \frac{2}{15}$$
$$= \frac{1}{15}$$

8. $2\frac{1}{3} - 5\frac{4}{9} = 2 + \frac{1}{3} - 5 - \frac{4}{9}$

$$= 2 - 5 + \frac{1}{3} - \frac{4}{9}$$
$$= -3 + \frac{3}{9} - \frac{4}{9}$$
$$= -3 + \frac{-1}{9}$$
$$= -3\frac{1}{9}$$

9. $\frac{3}{18} - \frac{5}{6} - \frac{2}{9} = \frac{3}{18} - \frac{5 \cdot 3}{6 \cdot 3} - \frac{2 \cdot 2}{9 \cdot 2}$

$$= \frac{3}{18} - \frac{15}{18} - \frac{4}{18}$$
$$= \frac{3 - 15 - 4}{18}$$
$$= \frac{-16}{9}$$
$$= -\frac{8}{9}$$

10. $-1\frac{7}{12}$ **11.** $-\frac{2}{3}$

12. a) $\left(14\frac{4}{5} - 12\frac{1}{10}\right)$ in.

     b) $2\frac{7}{10}$ in.

13. $7\frac{1}{8}$ ft

14. $1\frac{1}{6}$ in.

15. $5\frac{2}{3}$ ft

16. $-\frac{3}{7} \cdot \frac{7}{12} = \frac{-3 \cdot 7}{7 \cdot 12}$

$$= \frac{-\overset{1}{\cancel{3}} \cdot \overset{1}{\cancel{7}}}{\underset{1}{\cancel{7}} \cdot \underset{4}{\cancel{12}}}$$
$$= -\frac{1}{4}$$

17. $\left(-3\frac{2}{3}\right) \cdot 2\frac{2}{5} = -\frac{\boxed{11}}{3} \cdot \frac{\boxed{12}}{5}$

$$= \frac{-11 \cdot \overset{4}{\cancel{12}}}{\underset{1}{\cancel{3}} \cdot 5}$$
$$= -\frac{44}{5}$$
$$= -8\frac{4}{5}$$

18. $-\frac{3}{14}$ **19.** $7\frac{1}{5}$

20. $\dfrac{9}{20} \div \left(-\dfrac{3}{35}\right) = \dfrac{9}{20} \cdot \left(-\dfrac{\boxed{35}}{3}\right)$

$\qquad = \dfrac{-\,^3\cancel{9} \cdot \cancel{35}^{\,7}}{^4\,20 \cdot \cancel{3}^{\,1}}$

$\qquad = \dfrac{-21}{4}$

$\qquad = \underline{-5\dfrac{1}{4}}$

21. $\dfrac{\left(\dfrac{1}{2}\right)}{\left(-\dfrac{3}{10}\right)} = \dfrac{1}{2} \div \left(-\dfrac{3}{10}\right)$

$\qquad = \dfrac{1}{2} \cdot \left(-\dfrac{\boxed{10}}{3}\right)$

$\qquad = \dfrac{1 \cdot \left(-\cancel{10}^{\,5}\right)}{_2\cancel{2} \cdot 3}$

$\qquad = \dfrac{-5}{3}$

$\qquad = \underline{-1\dfrac{2}{3}}$

22. $-\dfrac{3}{8}$ **23.** $-3\dfrac{3}{4}$

24. $-1\dfrac{1}{2}$ **25.** -2

Lesson 2.6

1. $\underline{-4.09} - \underline{3.62} = \underline{4.09} - \underline{3.62}$
$\qquad\qquad\qquad = \underline{0.47}$
$3.62 + (-4.09) = \underline{-0.47}$

2. 1.74 **3.** -5.7

4. $70.5 - \underline{10.9} + \underline{12.1}$
$\quad = \underline{59.6} + \underline{12.1}$
$\quad = \underline{71.7}$
The final temperature is $\underline{71.7}$°F.

5. 9.56 ft **6.** -3.9°F

7. $\begin{array}{r} {}^5{}1{}^1 9.3 \\ \times\quad 0.6 \\ \hline 1\,1\,5\,8 \\ 0\,0\,0 \\ \hline 1\,1.5\,8 \end{array}$

$19.3 \cdot (-0.6) = \underline{-11.58}$

8. -3.234 **9.** 14.84

10. -70.99 **11.** $\$0.76$

12. $(-23.49) \div 0.9 = \underline{-234.9} \div 9$
$\qquad\qquad\qquad\quad = \underline{-26.1}$

$\begin{array}{r} 26.1 \\ 9\overline{)234.9} \\ \underline{18} \\ 54 \\ \underline{54} \\ 9 \\ \underline{9} \\ 0 \end{array}$

13. -7.1 **14.** -0.9
15. -81.7 **16.** -45.8

17. $(4.5 \cdot \underline{20}) - (\underline{2.1} \cdot 10) = \underline{90} - \underline{21}$
$\qquad\qquad\qquad\qquad\qquad = \underline{69}$
The change in altitude is $\underline{69}$ feet.

18. **Method 1**
$\$58 + (\underline{0.04 \cdot \$58}) = \$58 + \underline{\$2.32}$
$\qquad\qquad\qquad\quad = \underline{\$60.32}$
The cost of the tennis racket is $\underline{\$60.32}$.
Method 2
$\$58 \cdot \underline{1.04} = \underline{\$60.32}$
The cost of the tennis racket is $\underline{\$60.32}$.

19. -43 ft **20.** $\$18.90$

21. Percent change:
$\dfrac{\boxed{1.92} - \boxed{2.4}}{2.4} \cdot 100\% = \dfrac{(-0.48)}{2.4} \cdot 100\%$
$\qquad\qquad\qquad\qquad = \underline{-20\%}$
The percent change in the city's population is $\underline{-20\%}$.

22. About -0.55% **23.** About 23.77%

Chapter 3

Lesson 3.1
1. 2 **2.** 2
3. 5 **4.** $+$
5.

x	$x + 7$	$5x$	$3x - 1$
-1	6	-5	-4
0	7	0	-1
-2	5	-10	-7
5	12	25	14

6. Cannot be simplified.
7. $2g$ **8.** $10n + 2$
9. $6p$ **10.** $3x + 6$
11. $10 + 15m$ **12.** $8y - 14$
13. $28 - 21p$ **14.** $2(n + 3)$
15. $3(2x + 3)$ **16.** $5(2p - 1)$
17. $3(4 - 5y)$ **18.** **b)** $3(3m - 4)$

19. $x - 3$ **20.** $7x$

21. $2x + 2$ **22.** $\frac{1}{3}x - 8$

23.

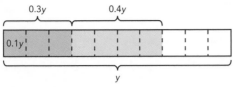

From the bar model,

$0.3y + 0.4y = \underline{0.7y}$

24. $0.4m$ **25.** $1.3h$

26. x **27.** $1.7g$

28. Method 1

Use a bar model.

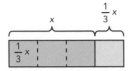

From the bar model,

$x + \frac{1}{3}x = \underline{\frac{4}{3}x}$

Method 2

Rewrite the coefficients.

$x + \frac{1}{3}x = \underline{\frac{3}{3}}x + \frac{1}{3}x$

$= \underline{\frac{4}{3}}x$

29. $\frac{6}{5}x$ **30.** $\frac{9}{7}b$

31. Method 1

Use a bar model.

$\frac{1}{3}x = \underline{\frac{2}{6}}x \quad \frac{1}{6}$

From the bar model,

$\frac{1}{3}x + \frac{1}{6}x = \underline{\frac{3}{6}}x$

$= \underline{\frac{1}{2}}x$

Method 2

Rewrite the coefficients.

$\frac{1}{3}x + \frac{1}{6}x = \underline{\frac{2}{6}}x + \frac{1}{6}x$

$= \underline{\frac{3}{6}}x$

$= \underline{\frac{1}{2}}x$

32. $\frac{5}{6}p$ **33.** $\frac{4}{5}d$

34. $\frac{19}{15}k$ **35.** $\frac{11}{12}y$

36. $\frac{17}{15}a$ **37.** $\frac{13}{18}w$

Lesson 3.2

1.

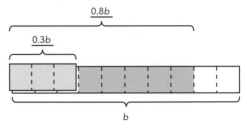

$0.8b - 0.3b = \underline{0.5b}$

2. $0.8a$ **3.** $4.1g$

4. $0.4h$ **5.** $0.5p$

6. Method 1

Use a bar model.

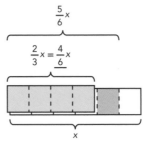

From the bar model,

$\frac{5}{6}x - \frac{2}{3}x = \underline{\frac{1}{6}}x$

Method 2

Rewrite the coefficients.

$\frac{5}{6}x - \frac{2}{3}x = \frac{5}{6}x - \underline{\frac{4}{6}}x$

$= \underline{\frac{1}{6}}x$

7. *Method 1*

Use a bar model.

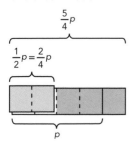

From the bar model,

$$\frac{5}{4}p - \frac{1}{2}p = \underline{\frac{3}{4}}p$$

Method 2

Rewrite the coefficients.

$$\frac{5}{4}p - \frac{1}{2}p = \frac{5}{4}p - \underline{\frac{2}{4}}p$$
$$= \underline{\frac{3}{4}}p$$

8. $\frac{3}{8}x$

9. $\frac{11}{18}y$

10. $\frac{1}{12}m$

11. $\frac{5}{24}d$

12. $\frac{5}{8}k$

13. $\frac{7}{10}w$

Lesson 3.3

1. $\underbrace{1.3x + 3x}_{} + 4$

$$= \underline{4.3x} + \underline{4}$$

2. $\underbrace{1.7y - 0.8y}_{} - 3$

$$= \underline{0.9y} - \underline{3}$$

3. $2.1f + 5$

4. $2.5g - 2$

5. $\frac{3}{5}y - \frac{3}{10}y - 1 + 3$

$$= \underline{\frac{6}{10}}y - \frac{3}{10}y - 1 + 3$$

$$= \underline{\frac{3}{10}}y + \underline{2}$$

6. $\frac{2}{3}d - \frac{1}{4}d - 2 - 5$

$$= \underline{\frac{8}{12}}d - \underline{\frac{3}{12}}d - 2 - 5$$

$$= \underline{\frac{5}{12}}d - \underline{7}$$

7. $1.6x + 0.5x - 0.8x$

$$= \underline{2.1x} - 0.8x$$

$$= \underline{1.3x}$$

8. $\frac{2}{7}y + \frac{1}{14}y + \frac{5}{7}y$

$$= \underline{\frac{4}{14}}y + \frac{1}{14}y + \underline{\frac{10}{14}}y$$

$$= \underline{\frac{5}{14}}y + \underline{\frac{10}{14}}y$$

$$= \underline{\frac{15}{14}}y$$

9. $2.3m$

10. $3.5g$

11. $\frac{2}{3}s$

12. $\frac{1}{6}c$

13. $6b + 4 + 7b + 9$

$$= \underline{6b} + \underline{7b} + 4 + 9$$

$$= \underline{13b} + \underline{13}$$

14. $\frac{4}{9}d + \frac{2}{7} - \frac{2}{9}d - \frac{1}{7}$

$$= \underline{\frac{4}{9}}d - \underline{\frac{2}{9}}d + \underline{\frac{2}{7}} - \underline{\frac{1}{7}}$$

$$= \underline{\frac{2}{9}}d + \underline{\frac{1}{7}}$$

15. $6n - 3$

16. $\frac{5}{7}f + \frac{2}{7}$

17. $8d + 9w + d + 8w$

$$= (\underline{8d} + \underline{d}) + (\underline{9w} + \underline{8w})$$

$$= \underline{9d} + \underline{17w}$$

18. $9a + 3b$

19. $4x + 2y$

20. $13g + 4h$

21. $4p - 6r$

Lesson 3.4

1. *Method 1*

Use a bar model.

| 4x + 6 | 2x | 3 | 2x | 3 |

$$\frac{1}{2}(4x + 6)$$

From the bar model,

$$\frac{1}{2}(4x + 6) = \underline{2x} + \underline{3}$$

Method 2

Use the distributive property.

$$\frac{1}{2}(4x + 6) = \frac{1}{2}(\underline{4x}) + \frac{1}{2}(\underline{6})$$

$$= \underline{2x} + \underline{3}$$

2. $3x + 4$

3. $2x + 7$

4. $\frac{8}{3}m + 2$

5. $\frac{7}{8} + \frac{3}{8}n$

6. $0.3 (3x + 7)$

$= 0.3(3x + 7)$

$= 0.3(\underline{3x}) + 0.3(\underline{7})$

$= \underline{0.9x} + \underline{2.1}$

7. $1.89y - 1.8$

8. $0.6p + 3.15$

9. $3.9w - 1.43$

10. $-3(-5a - 6)$

$= -3[-5a + (\underline{-6})]$

$= -3(\underline{-5a}) + (-3)(\underline{-6})$

$= \underline{15a + 18}$

11. $-\dfrac{1}{4}(4y + 7)$

$= -\dfrac{1}{4}(\underline{4y}) + \left(-\dfrac{1}{4}\right)(\underline{7})$

$= \underline{-y} + \left(\underline{-\dfrac{7}{4}}\right)$

$= \underline{-y - \dfrac{7}{4}}$

12. $-6x - 1$

13. $-\dfrac{3}{2}a + 10$

14. $2x - \dfrac{1}{6}$

15. $4.2x + 5.4$

16. $4(2d + 3f) + 6d$

$= 4(\underline{2d}) + 4(\underline{3f}) + \underline{6d}$

$= \underline{8d} + \underline{12f} + \underline{6d}$

$= \underline{8d} + \underline{6d} + \underline{12f}$

$= \underline{14d} + \underline{12f}$

17. $4g + 23h$

18. $9x + 21y$

19. $-2(1.5y - 1) - 2y$

$= -2[1.5y + (\underline{-1})] - 2y$

$= -2(\underline{1.5y}) + (-2)(-1) - \underline{2y}$

$= \underline{-3y} + \underline{2} - \underline{2y}$

$= \underline{-3y} - \underline{2y} + \underline{2}$

$= \underline{-5y} + \underline{2}$

20. $-4g + 8$

21. 12

22. $3(2a + 4) - 2(b - 2)$

$= 3(2a + 4) + (\underline{-2})(b - \underline{2})$

$= 3(\underline{2a}) + 3(\underline{4}) + (\underline{-2})(b) + (\underline{-2})(\underline{-2})$

$= \underline{6a} + \underline{12} + (\underline{-2b}) + \underline{4}$

$= \underline{6a} + (\underline{-2b}) + \underline{12} + \underline{4}$

$= \underline{6a} - \underline{2b} + \underline{16}$

23. $2x - y - 16$

24. $-2m - 4n + 12$

25. $3d - 6g + 25$

26. $-6p - 5q + 22$

Lesson 3.5

1. $3a - 15b$

$= \underline{3a} + (\underline{-15b})$

$= \underline{3}(\underline{a}) + \underline{3}(\underline{-5b})$

$= \underline{3}(\underline{a - 5b})$

2. $3(x - 4y)$

3. $7(m - 3n)$

4. $-4x - 7$

$= -4x + (\underline{-7})$

$= \underline{-1}(\underline{4x}) + (\underline{-1})(\underline{7})$

$= \underline{-1}(\underline{4x + 7})$

$= \underline{-(4x + 7)}$

5. $-8a - 12b$

$= \underline{-8a} + (\underline{-12b})$

$= \underline{-4}(\underline{2a}) + (\underline{-4})(\underline{3b})$

$= \underline{-4}(\underline{2a + 3b})$

6. $-(3x + 1)$

7. $-(5 + 4m)$

8. $-3(2a + 3b)$

9. $-4(m + 3n)$

Lesson 3.6

1. $\underbrace{5x}$ shared among $\underbrace{4}$

$\underbrace{5x \qquad\qquad \div \qquad\qquad 4}$

$\dfrac{5x}{4}$

Each sponge cake requires $\dfrac{5x}{4}$ pounds of flour.

2. $\underbrace{w}$ increased by $\underbrace{30\%}$

$\underbrace{\qquad\qquad\qquad\qquad \dfrac{30\% \text{ of } w}{=}}$

$\underbrace{w \qquad\qquad + \qquad\qquad 0.3\,w}$

$\underline{w + 0.3w}$

$= \underline{1.3w}$

He sold the watch for $\underline{1.3w}$ dollars.

3. $\dfrac{17}{30}x$ dollars

4. Perimeter of the triangle:

$\underline{3x} + \left(\dfrac{1}{4}x + 3\right) + \left(\dfrac{1}{4}x + 3\right)$

$= \left(\underline{\dfrac{7}{2}x + 6}\right)$

The perimeter of the triangle is $\left(\underline{\dfrac{7}{2}x + 6}\right)$ inches.

5. $(165x - 200)$ dollars

6. $(197x + 98y)$ dollars

7. $\left(\dfrac{x}{5} - 8\right)$ dollars

Lesson 3.7

1. $5\left(\dfrac{1}{8}y + 8\right)$

$= \underline{5}\left(\dfrac{1}{8}y\right) + \underline{5}(\underline{8})$

$= \dfrac{5}{8}y + \underline{40}$

He walked and jogged a total distance of

$\left(\dfrac{5}{8}y + 40\right)$ miles.

2. $(21x + 3.5)$ cm

3. $\left(\dfrac{6}{5}x + 9\right)$ cm²

4. $\left(14 - \dfrac{2}{7}p\right)$ pencils

5. Total sum of money:

$2m + \left(\dfrac{3m}{2}d - 5\right) + \left(\dfrac{3m}{2} - 5 + \dfrac{m}{6}\right)$

$= 2m + \dfrac{3}{2}m - 5 + \dfrac{3}{2}m - 5 + \dfrac{1}{6}m$

$= 2m + \dfrac{3}{2}m + \dfrac{3}{2}m + \dfrac{1}{6}m - 5 - 5$

$= \dfrac{12}{6}m + \dfrac{9}{6}m + \dfrac{9}{6}m + \dfrac{1}{6}m - 5 - 5$

$= \dfrac{31}{6}m - 10$

The total sum of money Adeline, Bill, and Celia

have is $\left(\dfrac{31}{6}m - 10\right)$ dollars.

6. $(x - 15)$ books

7. $\left(4x + \dfrac{5}{6}q - 40\right)$ passengers

8. $(7m + 8.4w)$ dollars

9. $\left(\dfrac{3}{2}p + q\right)$ pears and oranges

Chapter 4

Lesson 4.1

1. $x = 2$ 　　　　**2.** $x = \dfrac{5}{2}$

3. $y = 6$ 　　　　**4.** $y = \dfrac{3}{5}$

5. True 　　　　**6.** True

7. True 　　　　**8.** False

9.

10.

11.

12.

13. $x \le 15$ 　　　　**14.** $x \ge 18$

15. $x \le 20$ 　　　　**16.** $x > 30$

17. $2x - 1 + 3x = 4$

$5x - 1 = 4$

$5x - 1 + \underline{1} = 4 + \underline{1}$

$5x = \underline{5}$

Because $2x - 1 + 3x = 5$ _can_ be rewritten as $5x = 5$, the equations are _equivalent_.

18. $3x = 15$

$3x \div \underline{3} = 15 \div \underline{3}$

$x = \underline{5}$

Then check to see if $\underline{5}$ is the solution of the

equation $\dfrac{3}{5}x = 6$.

If $x = \underline{5}$, $\dfrac{3}{5}x = \dfrac{3}{5} \cdot \underline{5}$

$= \underline{3}$

Because the equations have _different_ solutions,

they are _not equivalent_ equations. So, $\dfrac{3}{5}x = 6$ and

$3x = 15$ are _not equivalent_ equations.

19. Yes, because $4x + 1 - 2x = 7$ can be rewritten as $x = 3$.

20. No, because the equations have different solutions.

Lesson 4.2

1. $6 + 8x = 24$

$6 + 8x - \underline{6} = 24 - \underline{6}$

$8x = \underline{18}$

$8x \div \underline{8} = \underline{18} \div \underline{8}$

$x = \dfrac{9}{4}$

$x = \dfrac{9}{4}$ gives the solution of the equation

$6 + 8x = 24$.

Check: Substitute the value of $x = \dfrac{9}{4}$ into the original equation.

$6 + 8x = 6 + 8 \cdot \dfrac{9}{4}$

$= 6 + 18$

$= \underline{24}$

When $x = \dfrac{9}{4}$, the equation $6 + 8x = 24$ is true.

So $x = \dfrac{9}{4}$ gives the solution.

2. $x = -\dfrac{4}{3}$ **3.** $y = -3$

4. Method 1

Solve by balancing the equation.

$$\dfrac{1}{3}x + \dfrac{1}{6} = \dfrac{1}{2}$$

$$\dfrac{1}{3}x + \dfrac{1}{6} - \underline{\dfrac{1}{6}} = \dfrac{1}{2} - \underline{\dfrac{1}{6}}$$

$$\dfrac{1}{3}x = \underline{\dfrac{1}{3}}$$

$$\underline{3} \cdot \left(\dfrac{1}{3}x\right) = \underline{\dfrac{1}{3}} \cdot \underline{3}$$

$$x = \underline{1}$$

Method 2

Solve by multiplying the equation by the least common denominator (LCD).

$$\dfrac{1}{3}x + \dfrac{1}{6} = \dfrac{1}{2}$$

$$\underline{6} \cdot \left(\dfrac{1}{3}x + \dfrac{1}{6}\right) = \underline{6} \cdot \left(\dfrac{1}{2}\right)$$

$$\underline{6} \cdot \dfrac{1}{3}x + \underline{6} \cdot \dfrac{1}{6} = \underline{6} \cdot \left(\dfrac{1}{2}\right)$$

$$2x + \underline{1} = \underline{3}$$

$$2x + \underline{1} - \underline{1} = \underline{3} - \underline{1}$$

$$2x = \underline{2}$$

$$2x \div \underline{2} = \underline{2} \div \underline{2}$$

$$x = \underline{1}$$

$x = \underline{1}$ gives the solution of $\dfrac{1}{3}x + \dfrac{1}{6} = \dfrac{1}{2}$.

Check: Substitute $\underline{1}$ for x into the original equation.

$$\dfrac{1}{3}x + \dfrac{1}{6} = \dfrac{1}{2} = \dfrac{1}{3} \cdot \underline{1} + \dfrac{1}{6} = \dfrac{1}{2}$$

When $x = \underline{1}$, the equation $\dfrac{1}{3}x + \dfrac{1}{6} = \dfrac{1}{2}$ is true.

$x = \underline{1}$ gives the solution.

5. $x = \dfrac{1}{4}$

6. $w = -\dfrac{15}{16}$

7. $0.4x - 3 + 1.2x = 0.6$

$$\underline{1.6x} - 3 = 0.6$$

$$\underline{1.6x} - 3 + \underline{3} = 0.6 + \underline{3}$$

$$\underline{1.6x} = \underline{3.6}$$

$$\dfrac{1.6x}{1.6} = \dfrac{3.6}{1.6}$$

$$x = \underline{2.25}$$

8. $x = 3$

9. $y = 8.5$

10. $10 - 4x - \underline{2x} = 2x + 16 - \underline{2x}$

$$10 - \underline{6x} = 16$$

$$10 - \underline{6x} - \underline{10} = 16 - \underline{10}$$

$$\underline{-6x} = 6$$

$$\dfrac{-6x}{-6} = \dfrac{6}{-6}$$

$$x = \underline{-1}$$

11. $x = 3$ **12.** $y = -\dfrac{6}{5}$

13. $y = 2$ **14.** $p = -\dfrac{1}{3}$

15. $m = -\dfrac{1}{15}$ **16.** $w = 2$

17.

$$\dfrac{2}{7}y + 1 = \dfrac{3}{14}y - \dfrac{1}{2}$$

$$\dfrac{2}{7}y + 1 - \underline{\dfrac{3}{14}y} = \dfrac{3}{14}y - \dfrac{1}{2} - \underline{\dfrac{3}{14}y}$$

$$\underline{\dfrac{4}{14}}y + 1 - \underline{\dfrac{3}{14}}y = -\dfrac{1}{2}$$

$$\dfrac{1}{14}y + 1 = -\dfrac{1}{2}$$

$$\dfrac{1}{14}y + 1 - \underline{1} = -\dfrac{1}{2} - \underline{1}$$

$$\dfrac{1}{14}y = -\underline{\dfrac{3}{2}}$$

$$\underline{14} \cdot \left(\dfrac{1}{14}y\right) = \underline{14} \cdot \left(-\underline{\dfrac{3}{2}}\right)$$

$$y = \underline{-21}$$

18.

$$\dfrac{1}{10}x - \dfrac{2}{5} = \dfrac{3}{4}x + \dfrac{1}{4}$$

$$\underline{20} \cdot \left(\dfrac{1}{10}x - \dfrac{2}{5}\right) = \underline{20} \cdot \left(\dfrac{3}{4}x + \dfrac{1}{4}\right)$$

$$\underline{20} \cdot \dfrac{1}{10}x - \underline{20} \cdot \dfrac{2}{5} = \underline{20} \cdot \dfrac{3}{4}x + \underline{20} \cdot \dfrac{1}{4}$$

$$2x - \underline{8} = 15x + 5$$

$$2x - \underline{8} - \underline{2x} = 15x + 5 - \underline{2x}$$

$$-8 = \underline{13x} + 5$$

$$-8 - 5 = \underline{13x} + 5 - \underline{5}$$

$$-13 = \underline{13x}$$

$$\dfrac{-13}{13} = \dfrac{13x}{13}$$

$$\underline{-1} = x$$

19. $p = 4$

20. $y = \dfrac{3}{25}$

21. $\dfrac{1}{3}(2y + 6) = 3$

$$\underline{3} \cdot \dfrac{1}{3}(2y + 6) = \underline{3} \cdot 3$$

$$2y + \underline{6} = 9$$

$$2y + \underline{6} - \underline{6} = 9 - \underline{6}$$

$$\underline{2y} = \underline{3}$$

$$\dfrac{2y}{2} = \dfrac{3}{2}$$

$$y = \underline{\dfrac{3}{2}}$$

22. $x = 6$

23. $m = -1$

24.
$$2x + 4(6 - x) = 30$$
$$2x + 4 \cdot \underline{6} - 4 \cdot \underline{x} = 30$$
$$2x + \underline{24} - \underline{4x} = 30$$
$$\underline{-2x} + \underline{24} = 30$$
$$\underline{-2x} + \underline{24} - \underline{24} = 30 - \underline{24}$$
$$\underline{-2x} = \underline{6}$$
$$\frac{-2x}{-2} = \frac{6}{-2}$$
$$x = \underline{-3}$$

25. $y = 1$ **26.** $p = 7$

Lesson 4.3

1.
$$\underline{y} + \frac{2}{3}y = -30$$
$$\frac{5}{3}y = -30$$
$$\frac{3}{5} \cdot \frac{5}{3}y = \frac{3}{5} \cdot (-30)$$
$$y = \underline{-18}$$

The other temperature:
$$\frac{2}{3}y = \frac{2}{3} \cdot \underline{-18} = \underline{-12}$$

The two measurements recorded were $\underline{-18}°C$ and $\underline{-12}°C$.

2. Melissa: 30; Elle: 15

3. Apples: 22; Oranges: 66

4. a)

Seats	Price	Number of Seats	Total Sale
Premiere	$120	375	45,000
Economical	$75	x	75x

From the table, the total amount of ticket sales is $\underline{(45,000 + 75x)}$ dollars.

b)
$$\underline{45,000} + \underline{75x} = 86,250$$
$$\underline{45,000} + \underline{75x} - \underline{45,000} = 86,250 - \underline{45,000}$$
$$\underline{75x} = \underline{41,250}$$
$$\frac{75x}{75} = \frac{41,250}{75}$$
$$x = \underline{550}$$

There were $\underline{550}$ tickets for economical seats sold.

5. a) $(205x + 275,000)$ dollars

   b) 1,100 front row seats

6. a) $(130y + 73,500)$ dollars

   b) 700 seats

7. Let Jasmine's score be y.

Then Jamie's score is $y + \underline{5}$.

Because they scored a total of 153 points,
$$y + (y + \underline{5}) = 153$$
$$\underline{2y} + \underline{5} = 153$$
$$\underline{2y} + \underline{5} - \underline{5} = 153 - \underline{5}$$
$$\underline{2y} = \underline{148}$$
$$\frac{2}{2}y = \frac{148}{2}$$
$$y = \underline{74}$$

Jamie's score: $y + \underline{5} = \underline{74} + \underline{5}$
$$= \underline{79}$$

Jamie scored $\underline{79}$ points on the test.

8. 36 years old

9. 20 min

Lesson 4.4

1.
$$1.9x + 2 + 0.1x \leq 5$$
$$\underline{2x} + 2 \leq 5$$
$$\underline{2x} + 2 - \underline{2} \leq 5 - \underline{2}$$
$$\underline{2x} \leq 3$$
$$\frac{2x}{2} \leq \frac{3}{2}$$
$$x \leq \frac{3}{2}$$

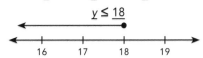

2. $m \geq 3$

3. $y < 1$

4.
$$-\frac{2}{7}y - 4 + \frac{9}{7}y \leq 14$$
$$\underline{y} - 4 \leq 14$$
$$\underline{y} - 4 + \underline{4} \leq 14 + \underline{4}$$
$$\underline{y \leq 18}$$

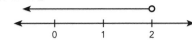

5. $x < 2$

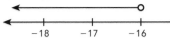

6. $w < -16$

7.

$$8 + \frac{3}{4}m > 11 - \frac{1}{4}m$$

$$8 + \frac{3}{4}m + \frac{1}{4}m > 11 - \frac{1}{4}m + \frac{1}{4}m$$

$$8 + \underline{m} > 11$$

$$8 + \underline{m} - \underline{8} > 11 - \underline{8}$$

$$\underline{m} > \underline{3}$$

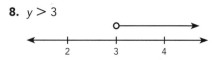

8. $y > 3$

9. $n \geq 6$

10. $1.5 > -0.3y$

$$\frac{1.5}{\boxed{-0.3}} \boxed{<} \frac{-0.3y}{\boxed{-0.3}}$$

$$\underline{-5} \boxed{<} y$$

11. $x < -12$

12. $x \leq -20$

13. $-2 - 2y < 7 + y$

$$-2 - 2y - y < 7 + y - y$$

$$-2 - \underline{3y} < 7$$

$$-2 - \underline{3y} + \underline{2} < 7 + \underline{2}$$

$$\underline{-3y} < \underline{9}$$

$$\frac{-3y}{\underline{-3}} > \frac{9}{\underline{-3}}$$

$$y > \underline{-3}$$

14. $x < -3$

15. $n < 5$

16. $2(2y + 5) > 6$

$$2(2y + 5) \div \underline{2} > 6 \div \underline{2}$$

$$\underline{2y} + 5 > \underline{3}$$

$$\underline{2y} + 5 - \underline{5} > \underline{3} - 5$$

$$\underline{2y} > \underline{-2}$$

$$\frac{2y}{\underline{2}} > \frac{-2}{\underline{2}}$$

$$y > \underline{-1}$$

17. $x < -7$

18. $x \geq -2$

Lesson 4.5

1. Average ≤ 40

$$\frac{30 + \underline{35} + \underline{35} + \underline{40} + \underline{x}}{5} \leq 40$$

$$\frac{140 + x}{5} \leq 40$$

$$5 \cdot \left(\frac{140 + x}{5}\right) \leq 5 \cdot 40$$

$$140 + \underline{x} \leq \underline{200}$$

$$140 + \underline{x} - \underline{140} \leq \underline{200} - 140$$

$$x \leq \underline{60}$$

The value of the fifth number is at most $\underline{60}$.

2. $18

3. 67

4. $2x + (\underline{-25 + x}) > 30$

$$2x - \underline{25} + \underline{x} > 30$$

$$\underline{3x} - \underline{25} > 30$$

$$3x - \underline{25} + \underline{25} > 30 + \underline{25}$$

$$\underline{3x} > \underline{55}$$

$$\frac{3x}{\underline{3}} > \frac{55}{\underline{3}}$$

$$x > 18\frac{1}{\underline{3}}$$

Kevin must get $\underline{19}$ correct answers in order to score more than $\overline{30}$ points.

5. 11 pens

6. 35 correct answers

7.
$$50 + \underline{80y} < 30 + \underline{100y}$$
$$50 + \underline{80y} - \underline{100y} < 30 + \underline{100y} - \underline{100y}$$
$$50 - \underline{20y} < 30$$
$$50 - \underline{20y} - \underline{50} < 30 - \underline{50}$$
$$\underline{-20y} < \underline{-20}$$
$$\frac{-20y}{-20} > \frac{-20}{-20}$$
$$y > \underline{1}$$

Best Movie Club will be less expensive than Ultimate Movie Club after $\underline{1}$ month(s).

8. Felicia can bring a maximum of 2 people for the tour.

9. Emily would have to exceed by 101 hours to incur more cost at Studio A than at Studio B.

Chapter 5

Lesson 5.1

1. Yes; 4 : 6 and 6 : 9
2. No; 2 : 3 and 12 : 18
3. Yes; 18 : 32 and 27 : 48
4. No; 2 : 5 and 20 : 50
5. No; 12 : 20 and 6 : 10
6. No; 18 : 8 and 9 : 4
7. No; 6 : 16 and 3 : 8
8. No; 5 : 3 and 15 : 9
9. Yes; 5
10. No   11. Yes; 8
12. For each pair of values, x and y:

$$\frac{14 \text{ h}}{2 \text{ cars}} = \underline{7} \quad \frac{21 \text{ h}}{3 \text{ cars}} = \underline{7} \quad \frac{28 \text{ h}}{4 \text{ cars}} = \underline{7}$$

Is the time taken to service each car directly proportional to the number of cars? $\underline{\text{Yes}}$

If so, what is the constant of proportionality? $\underline{7}$

What does this value represent?
It represents the time taken to service each car.

Write the direct proportion equation.
The direct proportion equation is $y = 7x$.

13. Yes; 9; $y = 9x$.
14. Yes; 5; $y = 5x$.
15.
$$3m = 5n$$
$$\boxed{\frac{1}{3}} \cdot 3m = 5n \cdot \boxed{\frac{1}{3}}$$
$$m = \frac{5}{3}n$$

Can the original equation $3m = 5n$ be written as an equivalent equation $m = \mathbf{k}n$? $\underline{\text{Yes}}$

Is the equation a direct proportion, and if so, what is the constant of proportionality?

Yes; The constant of proportionality is $\frac{5}{3}$.

16. Yes; 2
17. No

18. Constant of proportionality:

$$\frac{\boxed{26} \text{ points}}{\boxed{2} \text{ games}} = \underline{13}$$

The constant of proportionality is $\underline{13}$ and represents the points scored per game. The direct proportion equation is $\underline{P = 13m}$.

19. 5; It represents the number of books sold in an hour; $B = 5t$

20. $\frac{3}{4}$; It represents the number of red cars recorded per hour; $R = \frac{3}{4}t$

21. 60; It represents the distance traveled per minute; $D = 60x$

Lesson 5.2

1. Is the graph a straight line that passes through the origin? $\underline{\text{Yes}}$

So, does the graph represent a direct proportion? $\underline{\text{Yes}}$

Because the graph passes through point $(\underline{2}, \underline{10})$, the constant of proportionality is $\underline{5}$.
The direct proportion equation is $\underline{y = 5x}$.

2. Yes; 50; $y = 50x$
3. No.
4. Yes; 20; $y = 20x$
5. No.
6. **a)** Constant of proportionality: $\frac{4}{\underline{2}} = \underline{2}$

The constant of proportionality is $\underline{2}$. So, Jack serviced $\underline{2}$ air-conditioners per hour.

b) The direct proportion equation is $\underline{A = 2t}$.

c) It means that Jack services $\underline{6}$ air-conditioners in $\underline{3}$ hours.

d) From the graph, the number of air-conditioners serviced is $\underline{12}$.

e) From the graph, it takes him $\underline{4}$ hours to service 8 air-conditioners.

7. **a)** 2.5; 2.5 rooms
   b) $R = 2.5t$
   c) It means that Cheryl cleans 15 rooms in 6 hours.
   d) 20 rooms
   e) 4 h
8. **a)** 50; 50 balls
   b) $B = 50t$
   c) It means that 50 tennis balls are produced in 1 hour.
   d) 200 balls
   e) 2 h

Lesson 5.3

1. **a)** Constant of proportionality: $\frac{p}{r} = \frac{12}{\underline{3}} = \underline{4}$

The direct proportion equation is $p = \underline{4}r$.

b) *Method 1*

Use a proportion.

$$\frac{12}{3} = \frac{p}{\boxed{4}}$$

$$p \cdot 3 = 12 \cdot \underline{4}$$

$$3p = \underline{48}$$

$$\frac{3p}{3} = \frac{48}{3}$$

$$p = \underline{16}$$

Method 2

Use a direct proportion equation.

When $r = 4$ and $p = \underline{4}r$,

$$p = \underline{4} \cdot \underline{4}$$

$$p = \underline{16}$$

c) *Method 1*

Use a proportion.

$$\frac{12}{3} = \frac{\boxed{40}}{r}$$

$$12 \cdot r = \underline{40} \cdot \underline{3}$$

$$12r = \underline{120}$$

$$\frac{12r}{12} = \frac{120}{12}$$

$$r = \underline{10}$$

Method 2

Use a direct proportion equation.

When $p = 40$ and $p = \underline{4}r$,

$$40 = \underline{4}r$$

$$\frac{40}{4} = \frac{4r}{4}$$

$$\underline{10} = r$$

2. a) $m = 3n$　　　**b)** $m = 9$

　c) $n = 12$

3. a) $y = \frac{1}{2}x$　　**b)** $y = 4$

　c) $x = 50$

4. a) $s = \frac{2}{5}q$　　**b)** $s = 10$

　c) $q = 20$

5. a)

$$\frac{12}{4} = \frac{\boxed{18}}{x}$$

$$x \cdot 12 = 4 \cdot \underline{18}$$

$$12x = \underline{72}$$

$$\frac{12p}{\boxed{12}} = \frac{72}{12}$$

$$x = 6$$

b)

$$\frac{12}{4} = \frac{\boxed{y}}{10}$$

$$12 \cdot \underline{10} = y \cdot 4$$

$$\underline{120} = 4y$$

$$\frac{120}{4} = \frac{4y}{4}$$

$$\underline{30} = y$$

6. a) 4　　　　　　　**b)** 35

7. a) 12　　　　　　**b)** 4

8. a) 5　　　　　　　**b)** 98

9. a) Constant of proportionality:

$$\frac{n}{c} = \frac{360}{6} = \underline{60}$$

　　The constant of proportionality is $\underline{60}$.

　b) The direct proportion equation is $\underline{n = 60c}$.

　c) When $n = \underline{240}$ and $n = \underline{60} \cdot c$,

$$\underline{240} = \underline{60} \cdot c$$

$$\frac{240}{60} = \frac{60c}{60}$$

$$\underline{4} = c$$

10. a) 1.5　　　　　　**b)** $s = 1.5h$

　c) $s = 60$

11. a) 55 loaves of bread

　b) $N = 55T$　　　**c)** 6 h

12. a) 450 mi　　　　**b)** $d = 450t$

　c) 5 h

13. *Method 1*

Use a proportion.

Let y be the number of microchips produced.

$$\frac{\boxed{200} \text{ microchips}}{8 \text{ defective}} = \frac{y \text{ microchips}}{\boxed{33} \text{ defective}}$$

$$\frac{\boxed{200}}{8} = \frac{y}{\boxed{33}}$$

$$y \cdot 8 = \underline{200} \cdot \underline{33}$$

$$8y = \underline{6,600}$$

$$\frac{8y}{8} = \frac{6,600}{8}$$

$$y = \underline{825}$$

The factory produced $\underline{825}$ microchips.

Method 2

Use a direct equation proportion.

Let x be the number of defective microchips.

Let y be the number of microchips produced.

Constant of proportionality:

$$\frac{y}{x} = \frac{200}{8}$$

$$= \underline{25}$$

Direct proportion equation: $y = \underline{25}x$

When $x = \underline{33}$ and $y = \underline{25x}$, $y = \underline{25} \cdot \underline{33}$

$\qquad\qquad\qquad\qquad\quad y = \underline{825}$

The factory produced $\underline{825}$ microchips.

14. $18

15. 135 mg

16. 100 mg

17. *Method 1*

Use a proportion.

Let x be the percent decrease in the number of pairs of shoes Brandon sold.

$$\frac{100 \text{ percent}}{180 \text{ pairs of shoes}} = \frac{x \text{ percent}}{\boxed{45} \text{ pairs of shoes}}$$

$$\frac{100}{180} = \frac{x}{\boxed{45}}$$

$$x \cdot 180 = 100 \cdot \underline{45}$$

$$180x = \underline{4,500}$$

$$\frac{180x}{\boxed{180}} = \frac{4,500}{180}$$

$$x = \underline{25}$$

The percent decrease in the number of pairs of shoes Brandon sold is $\underline{25\%}$.

Method 2

Use a ratio.

Ratio of percents = Ratio of number of pairs of shoes sold

x percent : 100 percent = $\underline{45}$: $\underline{180}$

$$\frac{x}{100} = \frac{45}{180}$$

$$100 \cdot \frac{x}{100} = \frac{45}{180} \cdot \underline{100}$$

$$x = \underline{25}$$

The percent decrease in the number of pairs of shoes Brandon sold is $\underline{25\%}$.

18. 20%

19. 3%

20. 21%

Lesson 5.4

1.

x	2	3	6
y	18	12	6

For each pair of values, x and y:

$2 \cdot 18 = \underline{36}$ $3 \cdot 12 = \underline{36}$ $6 \cdot 6 = \underline{36}$

Is x inversely proportional to y? Yes

If yes, what is the constant of proportionality? $\underline{36}$

2.

x	2	5	15
y	25	10	3

For each pair of values, x and y:

$2 \cdot 25 = \underline{50}$ $5 \cdot 10 = \underline{50}$ $15 \cdot \underline{3} = \underline{45}$

Is x inversely proportional to y? No

If yes, what is the constant of proportionality? NA

3. Yes; 18 $\qquad\qquad$ **4.** No

5. Yes; 2

6. $\quad 3y = \dfrac{9}{x}$

$$3y \cdot \frac{1}{\underline{3}} = \frac{9}{x} \cdot \frac{1}{\underline{3}}$$

$$y = \frac{\boxed{3}}{x}$$

$$y \cdot x = \frac{3}{x} \cdot x$$

$$xy = \underline{3}$$

Can the original equation be written as two equivalent equations in the form $xy = k$ and $y = \dfrac{k}{x}$? Yes

Is the equation an inverse proportion, and if so, what is the constant of proportionality? Yes; 3

7. $\qquad y + 6x = 8$

$y + 6x - \underline{6x} = 8 - \underline{6x}$

$\qquad\quad y = \underline{8} - \underline{6x}$

Can the original equation be written as two equivalent equations in the form $xy = k$ and $y = \dfrac{k}{x}$? No

Is the equation an inverse proportion, and if so, what is the constant of proportionality? No

8. Yes; 2 $\qquad\qquad$ **9.** No

10. Yes; $\dfrac{1}{3}$.

11. Constant of proportionality:

$(1, 6) \longrightarrow 1 \cdot \underline{6} = \underline{6}$

The constant of proportionality is $\underline{6}$.

12. 9 $\qquad\qquad\qquad$ **13.** 12

14. 15 $\qquad\qquad\qquad$ **15.** 1

16. a) Use $(\underline{2}, \underline{8})$ to find the constant of proportionality:

$n \cdot t = \underline{2} \cdot \underline{8}$

$\qquad = \underline{16}$

The constant of proportionality is $\underline{16}$.

The inverse proportion equation is $\underline{nt = 16}$.

b) It means that $\underline{2}$ pipes can fill the swimming pool in $\underline{8}$ hours.

17. a) 150; $VP = 150$

b) It means that when there is 3 cubic meters of air in the balloon, the air pressure is 50 Newtons per square meter.

18. a) 24; $sn = 24$

b) It means that Sophie can cut 6 shorter pieces of rope if each piece measures 4 meters in length.

BLANK

BLANK

BLANK

BLANK

BLANK

BLANK

BLANK